W9-BKZ-078

Jane Austen

HAMLYN
London · New York · Sydney · Toronto

Brian Wilks
Jane Austen

'The whole aim of civilization is to make everything the source of enjoyment'

Tolstoy, *Anna Karenina*

'Nobody ever feels or acts, suffers or enjoys, as one expects.'
Jane Austen, *Letter to Cassandra 30 June 1808*

**For
my Mother and Father-in-law
Lily and Jonathan Hughes.
A small token of appreciation for
twenty-one very happy years.**

**Published by
Hammond Incorporated
Maplewood, New Jersey 07040**

© Copyright
The Hamlyn Publishing Group Limited 1978
All rights reserved. No part of this publication may be reproduced, stored in a retrieval system, or transmitted, in any form or by any means, electronic, mechanical, photocopying, recording or otherwise, without the prior permission of The Hamlyn Publishing Group Limited

ISBN 0-8437-3326-8
Phototypeset in England by Pilmtype Services Limited, Scarborough.
Printed in United States of America

title page: Chawton

Acknowledgments

I am grateful to the Jane Austen Society and the Jane Austen Memorial Trust for their kindness in allowing me to consult and reproduce material from their collections.

Any biographer of Jane Austen owes much to the painstaking work done by R. W. Chapman, whose edition of *Letters of Jane Austen to her sister Cassandra and Others* (Oxford 1952) is invaluable, and whose editions of Jane Austen's works, *The Oxford Illustrated Jane Austen* (Oxford 1954) in six volumes must be the standard text. All material quoted is from the Chapman edition. I was also very much helped by R. W. Chapman's *Jane Austen, Facts and Problems* (Oxford 1948) and his *Critical Bibliography* (Oxford 1953). In addition to the work of Chapman, I would like to express my gratitiude to that of B. C. Southam, whose *Jane Austen's Literary Manuscripts* (Oxford 1964) and his *Jane Austen, The Critical Heritage* were most helpful.

Among other biographies I would like to express my debt to Elizabeth Jenkins' *Jane Austen*, which must remain the finest biography and the most human and detailed, to Joan Rees, whose *Jane Austen Woman and Writer*, brings together so much accurate detail and reference material while telling the moving story of Jane Austen's life, and to Marghanita Laski, whose *Jane Austen and her world* helped me chart my way through the many relatives of the Austen family.

I must thank my daughter Jessica for cheerfully dictating letters and large pieces of eighteenth century prose; Jonathan for his friendship during a long preoccupation with yet another writer; and Marie who will understand the extent of my gratitude.

Finally I would like to record my appreciation of the help that I received from Margaret Offord, the most patient and long-suffering of editors, and Sheila Corr who not only searched for the pictures I asked for but struggled with my handwriting into the bargain.

Brian Wilks
Leeds, November 1977

Contents

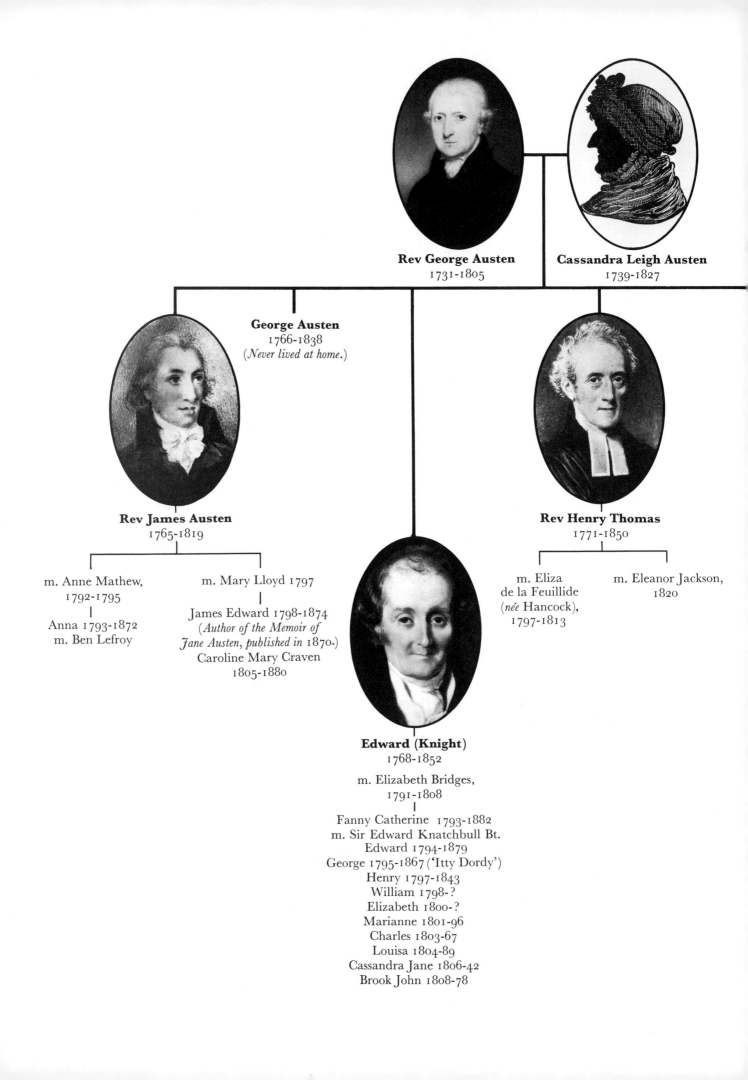

Rev George Austen
1731-1805

Cassandra Leigh Austen
1739-1827

George Austen
1766-1838
(*Never lived at home.*)

Rev James Austen
1765-1819

m. Anne Mathew,
1792-1795

Anna 1793-1872
m. Ben Lefroy

m. Mary Lloyd 1797

James Edward 1798-1874
(*Author of the Memoir of
Jane Austen, published in 1870.*)
Caroline Mary Craven
1805-1880

Rev Henry Thomas
1771-1850

m. Eliza
de la Feuillide
(*née* Hancock),
1797-1813

m. Eleanor Jackson,
1820

Edward (Knight)
1768-1852

m. Elizabeth Bridges,
1791-1808

Fanny Catherine 1793-1882
m. Sir Edward Knatchbull Bt.
Edward 1794-1879
George 1795-1867 ('Itty Dordy')
Henry 1797-1843
William 1798-?
Elizabeth 1800-?
Marianne 1801-96
Charles 1803-67
Louisa 1804-89
Cassandra Jane 1806-42
Brook John 1808-78

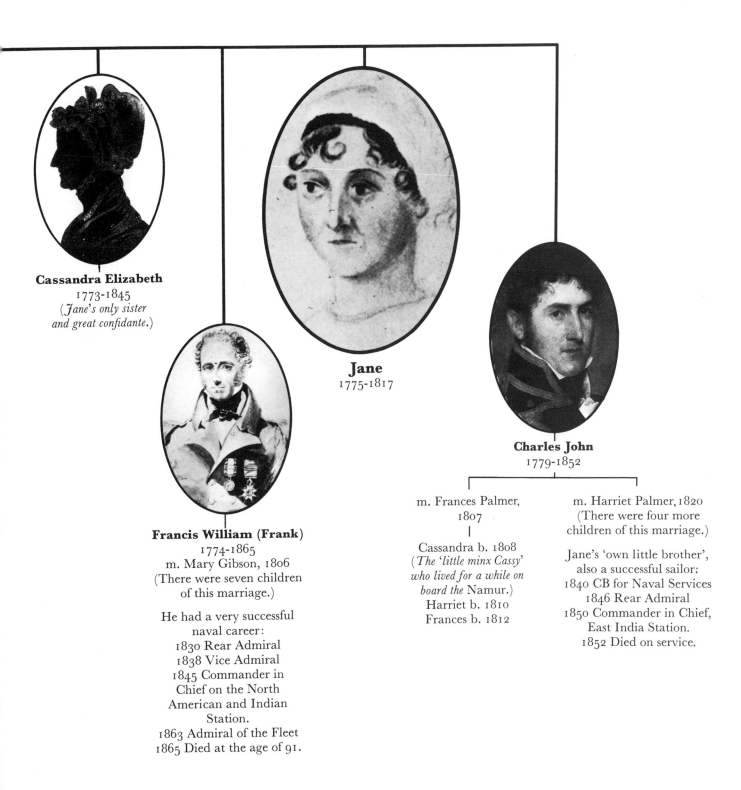

Cassandra Elizabeth
1773-1845
(*Jane's only sister
and great confidante.*)

Jane
1775-1817

Charles John
1779-1852

Francis William (Frank)
1774-1865
m. Mary Gibson, 1806
(There were seven children
of this marriage.)

He had a very successful
naval career:
1830 Rear Admiral
1838 Vice Admiral
1845 Commander in
Chief on the North
American and Indian
Station.
1863 Admiral of the Fleet
1865 Died at the age of 91.

m. Frances Palmer,
1807

Cassandra b. 1808
(*The 'little minx Cassy'
who lived for a while on
board the* Namur.)
Harriet b. 1810
Frances b. 1812

m. Harriet Palmer, 1820
(There were four more
children of this marriage.)

Jane's 'own little brother',
also a successful sailor:
1840 CB for Naval Services
1846 Rear Admiral
1850 Commander in Chief,
East India Station.
1852 Died on service.

Introduction:
The Eventful Life

ONE SEPTEMBER evening in 1813 a thirty-seven-year-old unmarried lady was to be found hurrying along a corridor with a pair of young gentleman's breeches hoping to transfer them from one bedroom to another without being caught halfway along the corridor between the two rooms. Earlier that year the same lady had seen her second novel published, and by the following November was to have the second edition of her first novel in her hand. The novels were *Sense and Sensibility* and *Pride and Prejudice*, the lady Miss Jane Austen:

> I wish you had seen Fanny and me running backwards and forwards with his Breeches from the little Chintz to the White room before we went to bed, in the greatest of frights lest he should come upon us before we had done it all – There had been a mistake in the Housemaids' Preparations and *they* were gone to bed.

In that brief lighthearted paragraph from a letter to her sister Cassandra in 1813 we can catch something of the nature of the lady whose humour, sensitivity and style were to combine to make her one of the most read, enjoyable and acclaimed prose writers in the whole of English literature.

Almost as soon as the first editions of *Sense and Sensibility* and *Pride and Prejudice* had sold out critics were noting their author's talent and already posing the now classic debate about Jane Austen's genius. The themes, characters, scope and preoccupations of her writing were recognized as different from other novelists, both male and female, and many critics found their discreet power and acute penetration of behaviour baffling.

Here were men and women that one recognized. Sir Walter Scott, in a review of Emma (sic) that delighted Jane Austen, confessed:

'A friend of ours, whom the author had never seen or heard of, was at once recognised by his own family as the original of Mr. Bennett, and we do not know if he has yet got rid of the nickname.' [Quarterly Review, 1816]

Shunning the swashbuckling heroes of romance and the swooning heroines of the haunted castle, Jane Austen created a world of recognizable people who have provided amusement for generations of readers and apparent exasperation for generations of students of literature. For some she is the 'first modern novelist'; for Tennyson she was 'a prose Shakespeare'; for others she is an infuriating miniaturist who ignored world issues to write of the 'uneventful' lives of small groups of genteel people. To Sir Walter Scott this was her unique strength:

'The narrative of all her novels is composed of such common occurrences as may have fallen under the observation of most folks; and her *dramatis personae* conduct themselves upon the motives and principles which the readers may recognise as ruling their own and that of most of their acquaintances.' [Ibid]

Ordinary people doing things that happen in everyday life: such, according to Scott, was the secret of Jane Austen's power. But the *common incidents* and the *ordinary nature* of Jane Austen's heroes and heroines, if indeed they are at all common and ordinary, led to a curious habit of mind among biographers and critics of Jane Austen's life and works. The word 'uneventful' became linked not only with her writing but also with her own life.

No one lives an uneventful life, and such a description denies the total circumstances of a given life in its setting. All lives are eventful and Jane Austen's was no exception. It is true that she was no Joan of Arc or Florence Nightingale, but her years abound with as much sorrow, disappointment and frustration as well as happiness, delight and success as any man's. As a member of a large well-educated and successful family, she understood much of the affairs of the world. Two of

Fort Belan, in Llanwnda, North Wales. A well-preserved example of a sea-defence built to protect the shores of Britain from the threat of attack from Napoleon. Fort Belan, begun in 1775, reminds us that in Boulogne there still stands a monument commemorating Napoleon's 'successful' invasion of England – an invasion that never took place. The threat of invasion was real, however, during Jane Austen's life, and this defence was built the same year as she was born.

'precision', do not display her entire way of life. Her life is not to be found in her novels and we are mistaken if we take their subtly controlled canvasses as the entire landscape of her forty-two years.

Jane Austen lived through an eventful period in English and European history, and her own life was also eventful and resonant with the interaction of personalities within and without her own family circle. For her, people mattered more than art, family more than literature.

When a friend whom she was to visit asked her what books she was going to bring with her, she received the following typical retort:

> You distress me cruelly by your request about books; I cannot think of any to bring with me, nor have I any idea of our wanting them. I come to you to be talked to, not to read or hear reading. I can do *that* at home; . . .

[Letter to Martha Lloyd, 12 November 1800]

The more one learns of Jane Austen's life the more it appears that she would have preferred to be remembered as a loving aunt than as a famous writer. The testimony of her nephews and nieces bears this out, and a charming letter to her niece Caroline, who at ten years had just become an aunt herself, indicates, albeit light-heartedly, her sense of good 'Auntship':

> Now that you are become an Aunt, you are a person of some consequence and must excite great Interest whatever you do. I have always maintained the importance of Aunts as much as possible, and am sure of your doing the same now,–Believe me my dear Sister-Aunt,
> Yours affectionately,
> J. Austen

[Letter to Caroline Austen, 30 October 1815]

Within the next fortnight, the 'Sister Aunt' was to be engaged in accepting the Prince Regent's invitation to dedicate her next novel to 'His Royal Highness'. Yet the busy and successful novelist still found time to humour her young niece, while incidentally setting out a tenet of her own philosophy.

The story of Jane Austen, novelist, is the story of a family and of a much loved member of that family. Against a background of social change and the growing impetus of the industrial revolution the story of her life chronicles the history of a Hampshire clergyman's family, recording in considerable detail their close involvement in one of the most formative periods of English history.

her older brothers became admirals in Nelson's navy, her eldest brother was adopted into the aristocracy and came to own and manage great houses, a cousin's husband fell victim to the revolutionary tribunal during the French Revolution and died under the guillotine, while her older brother George had to be nursed throughout his life and was never able to take his place with his brothers and sisters as a normal healthy person.

Jane Austen's artistic choices, those detailed works which Scott could praise for their 'elegance' and

England 1775-1817

ENGLAND was at war for all but seventeen of Jane Austen's forty-two years. In the July before she was born the Battle of Bunker Hill, the first pitched battle of the American War of Independence, was fought: she died only two years after the Battle of Waterloo. The war with America, the wars with France and Napoleon all happened during her lifetime and were important factors shaping the kind of world she knew, its concerns and its preoccupations. At times in a state of siege, at others fearing civil war and rebellion within her own shores, the British Isles knew the hardships and perils of a nation at war and could see how precarious the hold on civilization as she knew it could be. Rebellion was in the air. Many in England were to champion the cause of the French Revolution while America found its sympathizers in the London of George III. Like France and America, England was ripe for rebellion, for in the time of Jane Austen it was a land of high contrasts and gross inequality in living standards and conditions, between the nobility and gentry on the one hand and the common people on the other.

Throughout these stirring and troubled times, when Englishmen were volatile in politics and play, the British Navy won great victories which shielded the nation from the worst ravages of war. For the leisured classes the war was something that happened in the newspapers, or far out at sea. As Jane Austen herself remarked, as long as one knew none of the people involved in the fighting one's own peace could remain unruffled. However, Jane did know people that were involved as two of her brothers were naval officers for a period of some seventy-five years. Thus the wars were not as remote to her as they were for many. Her engagement in the pursuits of the leisured classes – her music, her painting and her writing – represent the activities of those shielded by the Royal Navy, those affairs of society that protected and secure wealthy

The Horsedrawn Carriage. *Jane Austen's world was dominated by the horse, its strengths and its weaknesses. Travel was unpredictable, uncomfortable, and at times exceedingly dangerous. More than one of Jane's close friends died as a result of an overturned carriage or from being thrown from a horse.*

people can enjoy.

Jane Austen's novels, her stories of young women fighting the battles of the heart to win the prize of marriage upon the field of courtship, belong as much to her times as do the lists of battle honours won by those involved in the nation's various war campaigns. While her brothers earned their living at the borders of civilization amid the horror of savage fighting, Jane Austen lived in the society that they and their fellow officers made possible. The contrast of the battlefield and the ballroom is apt as a reminder of the powerfully opposed elements that made up the England into which Jane Austen was born and in which she grew to maturity.

Despite the rumblings of the industrial and agricultural revolution that were to shift the centre of gravity for the whole of the civilized world, rumblings that steadily grew through each year of Jane Austen's life, England in the period 1775 to 1817 was still a rural, picturesque, agricultural society. The English landscapes of Turner, Constable and Stubbs bear witness to the unspoiled beauty that reached into the very towns themselves. The English countryside was serene, still heavily wooded, farmed and owned by aristocrats and landlords whose wealth increased during a series of boom years. Labour and servants were cheap, and the untroubled counties of England provided rich farmland. Many economic historians see the very years of Jane Austen's life as the hey-day of the English leisured class. Yet it was also a time of great contrast and social inequality. Elegance on the one hand, supported by the

best of the world's commodities, the best furniture, the finest silver, the best carriages; and on the other hand the unequal structure of a society where a third of the nation's population faced a daily struggle to survive. In the first part of the eighteenth century the greatest of the English stately homes were built and filled with the fruits of an expanding world market: French furniture, Italian paintings, Greek sculpture and Oriental china.

These homes and the great estates that went with them symbolize the hierarchical nature of English society at the time. From the monarch to the poorest of the land there was a pyramid of patronage and property. At the base of the pyramid, in 1803, a third of the population were the labouring poor, the cottagers, the seamen, the soldiers, the paupers and the vagrants, all of whom lived at subsistence level. Jane Austen's writing reveals the inequality of the times. In 1799, a time when a stable boy could be hired for four pounds a year, she wrote to her sister Cassandra of their brother's 'shopping' in Bath:

> He [Edward] made an important purchase yesterday; no less so than a pair of coach horses; his friend Mr Evelyn found them out and recommended them . . . Their colour is black and their size not large – their price sixty guineas . . .
> [Letter to Cassandra, 19 June 1799]

The contrast is clear. The horses cost sixty pounds, the stable boy to look after them, four. Such a contrast is echoed throughout the period in many different ways. The landscapes of Turner and Constable, those wooded hillsides and winding lanes amid gentle woodlands, offered man-traps and spring-guns which would kill and maim the unwary walker as well as the poacher. The

The Battle of Bunker Hill. The first pitched battle of the American War of Independence took place in the year of Jane Austen's birth. Revolution in France, revolution in America and the threat of revolution in Britain accompanied the elegance and mannered poise of late eighteenth-century life in England.

The Cornfield, by John Constable. This well-known landscape painting by Jane's contemporary shows an idealized rural scene which glosses over the real harshness of country life and the plight of the farm workers in times of famine and hardship when harvests failed.

harsh game laws which reserved hunting for the pleasure of a few amid a starving population—a man could be transported for seven years for merely possessing rabbit nets—were in force throughout Jane Austen's life. Her brother Edward, as an owner of great estates, would be directly involved.

The land of Turner and Constable was also the land of William Blake's chimney sweep, of Hogarth, Cruickshank and Rowlandson. The face of elegant society bore the pock marks of the smallpox epidemic.

The contrasts in England were also between tradition and technical innovation. The old world which depended upon a good harvest, a world where men were at the mercy of nature, was being challenged by the new. In time, with revolutionary methods in agriculture as well as new manufacturing processes, the harsh rule of nature would be softened. Jane Austen lived at a time when the forces that were to effect the change were collecting their strength. She died before the full impact of industrialization was evident but she lived in a society where the rumblings were to be heard and the first shocks to be felt. Writing with a quill, living by candle and oil-lamp, waiting upon her brother's carriages for transport, Jane Austen may have visited Trevithick's railway in Euston Square in 1809. The lady whose travels were dependent upon real horse power could have seen the power that was about to drive the modern world into being.

Jane Austen was three years old when Watt took out his patent for a steam engine to turn machinery, yet with only 500 such patents granted during her lifetime, it cannot be said that the industrial age had really begun. For Jane Austen as for those for whom she wrote it is the equestrian paintings of Stubbs that sum up the times, and if we would seek a symbol or emblem for them it must be the horse-drawn carriage rather than the steam engine. From the monarch to the modest farmer it was the muscles of beasts and men that organized the world in which Jane Austen lived. For many historians the year of her death (1817) is the end of an era. The great engineer and railway builder Brunel was ten years old, and in the next decade his work would begin.

Throughout this period the English aristocracy enjoyed a time of unprecedented pleasure and freedom. The troubles abroad, particularly in France, had led to much of Europe's greatness flowing into England. The hey-day of the leisured classes was made possible by

George Stubbs, Reapers, *1785. Stubbs portrays harvesting in an idyllic light, against a background of a serene, unspoiled and densely wooded landscape. We know from history, however, that the men and women who toiled at such occupations, so neatly and deftly portrayed here, would in reality have lived at bare subsistence level. Tate Gallery, London.*

JOHN BULL Happy.

JOHN BULL going to the WARS.

JOHN BULL'S Property in danger.

J.G.y des. et fecit.

JOHN BULL'S glorious Return.

JOHN BULL'S PROGRESS.

*This satirical cartoon by Gillray shows the 'progress'
of a 'typical' English family from relative affluence to
desperate poverty when the breadwinner leaves for the
Napoleonic wars. British Museum, London.*

sheer economic advantage. For Britain did not merely win the race for an international market; through technical innovation and the sheer genius of inventors and manufacturers it was able to remain some fifty years ahead of competitors. Rents increased and incomes for the wealthy soared. The years 1777 to 1800 saw the growth of sports and pastimes amongst the landed gentry, the rise of the spas and seaside resorts, and great interest in horse-racing, gambling and blood sports.

It was against this background that Jane Austen grew up and it is of the affairs of a particular section of that society that she wrote. Shunning the aristocracy and avoiding the dire plight of the poor, she wrote of the people whom she might have met in her own immediate circle. Of upper middle class parentage, it was of the upper middle classes that she wrote, wisely confining herself to that section of society that she knew well. Her genius was such that in portraying characters from that class she was able to examine the basis of human behaviour and its motivations. Her familiarity with her characters allowed her the most penetrating insight into the way we conduct our transactions with other people. Writing within her scope she created a world beyond most writers' capabilities. Her observations, however,

still arose from the nature of the society around her. It is the upper middle class in England under George III of which she writes.

All societies are the product of tension and conflict, and it is often at the times of greatest challenge that the character of an age can be most clearly seen. For the gentlefolk of Jane Austen's time this is arguably the case. The most distinct split in English society during this period was between the 'gentlefolk' and the common people. Long before the 'class' system became clearly divided into three distinct levels of upper, middle and working class—as symbolized by the introduction of first, second and third class carriages when railways came into being—the distinction most clearly to be seen was between those who worked by the sweat of their brow and those who did not:

'All are accounted gentlemen in England who maintain themselves without manual labour'.

There were, however, interesting subtleties within this definition. As 'gentlemen' were included Nobility, Gentry, Clergy, Physicians, Barristers and Overseas Merchants. The following were not automatically given 'gentleman' status: Dissenting Ministers, Apothecaries, Attornies, Schoolmasters, Professional Artists, and the

13

Inland Trader. The preoccupation of the 'gentleman' was to maintain a polite, polished world for which he needed the services of all those who stood beneath him in the social order.

In a picturesque and unspoiled countryside the threats of the future, like those of French invasion, could be considered but largely ignored. The ruling class had its protection in the form of a monopoly of world markets, secured by a fine navy abroad, and imposed poverty, game laws and difficulties in travelling and communications at home. This meant that the landed gentry could be happy being wealthy and could, as Trevelyan argues 'be engrossed in the life of their country houses'.

Jane Austen's family, by reason of her father being an Oxford scholar and a clergyman, were clearly 'gentle-folk'. It is not surprising, therefore, that it should be of 'gentlefolk' that she should write. It was not, however, merely an accident of birth that gave her her themes and artistic impetus. Being her father's daughter she was educated and provided with opportunity to do more than 'earn a living'. Being the person that she was she saw in her contemporaries in her own social group patterns of personal and communal behaviour that typify men and women living an agreeable life with all the necessities secured. She could explore the polite, polished society of well educated and 'civilized' people, for, until after her death in 1817, these were, together with the nobility whom they emulated, the only people who mattered in society.

Two writers, looking back on her time from the early part of the nineteenth century, show us clearly the fibre of the society in which she lived and from which she drew her material for her writing. Outlining the strength of English society Robinson (in *Blackwoods* in 1824) noted that despite the cleavage between 'gentlefolk' and common people, there were shades of grey:

'In most other countries, society presents scarcely anything but a void between an ignorant labouring population, and a needy profligate nobility . . . but with us the space between the ploughman and the peer, is crammed with circle after circle, fitted in the most admirable manner for sitting upon each other, for connecting the former with the latter, and for rendering the whole perfect in cohesion, strength and beauty.'

Robinson is here outlining that peculiar strength of English society, the strength that may have saved it from revolution in the eighteenth century: the closely-knit interdependent yet distinct social layers. Haydn, who when visiting England was astonished that it could be governed at all without a police force, failed to discern that the structure of family, village, great house, town, county and city, was so closely interwoven. It is of one particular 'circle' that Jane Austen was to write in her published novels: that of the gentry who were not quite nobility, but who certainly did not work for their living.

A further more complete view of the changes that were to take place in Jane Austen's lifetime comes from the *Collected Works of Rev Sydney Smith* who was only four years older than Jane Austen. Writing in retrospect in 1843 Smith reflects:

'It is of some importance at what period a man is born. A young man, alive at this period, hardly knows to what improvements of human life he has been introduced: and I would bring before his notice the following eighteen changes which have taken place in England since I first began to breathe in it the breath of life—a period amounting now to nearly seventy-three years. Gas was unknown: I groped about the streets of London in all but the utter darkness of a twinkling oil lamp, under the protection of watchmen in their grand climacteric and exposed to every species of depradation and insult.

I have been nine hours in sailing from Dover to Calais before the invention of steam. It took me nine hours to go from Taunton to Bath, before the invention of railroads, and now I go in six hours from Taunton to London. In going from Taunton to Bath, I suffered between 10,000 and 12,000 severe contusions, before stone-breaking Macadam was born.

I paid £15 in a single year for repairs to carriage springs on the pavements of London; and I now glide without noise or fracture, on wooden pavements.

I can walk, by the assistance of the police, from one end of London to the other, without molestation; or, if tired, get into a cheap and active cab, instead of those cottages on wheels, which the hackney carriages were at the beginning of my life.

I had no umbrella! They were little used, and very dear. There were no waterproof hats, and my hat has often been reduced by rains into its primitive pulp.

I could not keep my small clothes in their proper place, for braces were unknown. If I had gout there was no colchium. If I was bilious there was no calomel. If I was attacked by ague there was no quinine. There were filthy coffee houses instead of elegant clubs . . . There were no banks to receive the savings of the poor . . . whatever miseries I was suffering there was no post to whisk my complaints for a single penny to the remotest corners of the empire; and yet in spite of all these privations, I lived on quietly, and am now ashamed that I was not more discontented, and utterly surprised that all these changes and inventions did not occur two centuries ago.

I forgot to add that, as the basket of stagecoaches, in which luggage was then carried, had no springs, your clothes were rubbed all to pieces; and that even in the best society one third of the gentlemen at least were always drunk.'

A Hampshire Family

'We have now another girl'

JANE AUSTEN was born at Steventon in Hampshire on 16th December in the year 1775. The poet Wordsworth was four years old, Coleridge three and Southey one. Jane was a seventh child, the second daughter of a scholar-clergyman who was rector of the small country parishes of Steventon and Deane. Writing to announce her birth to a relative, her father George Austen was characteristically good humoured:

> You have doubtless been for some time in expectation of hearing from Hampshire, and perhaps wondered a little we were in our old age grown such bad reckoners but so it was, for Cassy certainly expected to have been brought to bed a month ago: however, last night the time came, and without a great deal of warning, everything was soon happily over. We have now another girl, a present plaything for her sister Cassy and a future companion.

Two years later another boy, Charles John, was to complete the family in which Jane lived.

The family was a healthy one. Jane's death in her forty-second year was an unusually early one for an Austen, though not for the times in which she lived. Five of her brothers lived long active lives while her sister Cassandra lived till she was seventy-three. There is one mystery that surrounds the family that has never been satisfactorily explained. The Austens' second son, George, born in 1766, never lived at home. We hear that he was subject to fits, and we know that money was paid for his keep. We can only guess at the nature of any handicap or malady he may have suffered. It is conjectured that he never returned from the wet-nurse to which it was customary to send children in the village, and that he was in some way abnormal. Jane Austen's ability to make herself understood using 'finger language' has been cited as evidence that George was perhaps a deaf mute. Be that as it may, the Austen family, for seventy-two years, provided for George to be cared for, and Jane had some insight into the implications of those many years.

'THE HANDSOME PROCTOR'

George Austen, Jane's father, came from an ancient family, albeit from a poor branch. His ancestors had been clothiers in the Middle Ages belonging to the 'Grey Coats of Kent', and in the sixteenth century they had been landowners. George Austen's grandmother however had been early left a widow with six children to bring up, the fourth of whom was William, Jane Austen's grandfather.

William became a surgeon in Tonbridge but both he and his wife died young leaving the six-year-old George in the care of his rich uncle Francis Austen. George Austen's humble beginnings and his rescue by a wealthy relative who continued to make provision for his young nephew was not an untypical transaction for the period. Families were acutely aware of the need in law and in tenure for close relationships and respect for kin. It was through such close alliance that estates were kept together and the fortunes of families remained intact. Sagacious adoption as well as conveniently 'arranged' marriages together with a true regard for family units that extended to cousins, nephews and nieces, were not at all uncommon as devices for security as well as expressions of familial affection. Kinship and dynastic concerns, as displayed in the educating and providing for George Austen, Jane's father, were to continue to have a bearing on the next generation of Austens throughout Jane's life, and to affect her standard of living.

Orphaned at six, Jane's father was well provided for by his wealthy Uncle Francis. Sent to Tonbridge Grammar School he then went on to St John's College Oxford where he distinguished himself by winning an open scholarship. From Oxford he returned to Tonbridge to teach in his old school where by 1758 he was second master. From schoolmastering he returned to Oxford as a fellow of St John's where he became known as 'the handsome proctor'. It was in 1760 that he took holy orders.

It was probably through the University that he met Cassandra Leigh whom he was to marry in Bath in 1764. Francis Austen's generous provision for his nephew – he already had children of his own to provide for – introduced George into a society for which he was admirably suited but otherwise would not have enjoyed. Able to live reasonably comfortably from his teaching he was, through his position at the college, and by way of his good looks, an eligible young man. Cassandra Leigh was very well connected at Oxford. Her uncle on her father's side was the celebrated if not legendary Dr Leigh, Master of Balliol College, a man renowned for his charm, elegance and wit. Cassandra's father was a clergyman and her ancestors included nobility. Sir Thomas Leigh, during the reign of Queen Elizabeth I, had been Lord Mayor of London while his son had sheltered Charles I at Stoneleigh Abbey during the civil war. Cassandra's father was exceptionally clever and had been a Fellow of All Souls at Oxford.

From this inheritance, Cassandra Leigh derived an originality of mind and confidence that seems to have made her more than usually mistress of herself. Little is reported of her except that she seems to have been contentedly herself, a presence to be accounted for in all family matters. The tradition is that she was a witty person, able to extemporize verse and tell stories of her own composing. We can be sure that in her own large family her education and background would serve her well. All accounts tell of the happiness of George and Cassandra Austen. We learn that they made a handsome couple.

Their marriage at Walcot Church in Bath signifies the long connection that the Austens of Hampshire were to have with that fine city. For not only were they married there, but many years later it would be in that graveyard that Jane's father would be buried. It was to

Bath that he retired in 1801 to live in the town where his brother-in-law James Leigh Perrot lived.

THE RECTORY AT STEVENTON

It was family connections that brought George Austen and his bride to live in Hampshire. Another rich relative, a distant but generous cousin, Thomas Knight of Godmersham in Kent, owned the living of the parish at Steventon and he was pleased to present it to George. Francis Austen, his previous benefactor, added to the first income by buying the living of Deane, a neighbouring parish, and presenting that to his nephew. The total income from the two livings was only modest, there being only some 300 souls living in the combined parishes. However, the livings were sufficient, a farm went with the Rectory at Steventon and through his schoolmastering George Austen was able to further increase his income. Thomas Knight who owned the living had rented out the manor house at Steventon, so that to all intents and purposes George Austen represented the family who owned the manor. This together with his office as rector led to him being to some extent seen as the equivalent of the lord of the manor.

At first the Austens lived in Deane, the small village next to Steventon. It was in 1771 that according to family tradition the Austens took up residence in the rectory where Jane was born; writing in his memoir of his aunt in 1870 J.E. Austen Leigh comments:
'The lane between Deane and Steventon has long been as smooth as the best turnpike road; but when the family removed from one residence to the other in 1771, it was a mere cart track, so cut up by deep ruts as to be impassable for a light carriage. Mrs Austen, who was not then in strong health, performed the journey on a feather-bed, placed upon some soft articles of furniture in the waggon which held their household goods.'
Today after two hundred years, and some changes, it is easy to visualize the lane along which the wagon passed. Steventon is still virtually buried in deep countryside, a tiny village where gentle wooded hills create a silence and shelter that enfolds as it shields.

About seven miles from Basingstoke, Steventon

The record of baptism for Jane Austen at Steventon in Hampshire, dated 17 December 1775.

village, like many other Hampshire villages, is a sprinkling of houses among trees along narrow lanes. The lanes can be closed avenues of trees or pass between open meadows. The countryside today is green and serene; in the Austens' day the woods must have been denser and more widespread and the lanes very rough and unreliable as thoroughfares. The whole effect of the landscape is to close in upon the inhabitants of the village. Here in the winter months people could be isolated for quite long spells. Communication was by foot or by horse and Jane's nephew describes the difficulties that in 1771 were commonplace:

'In those days it was not unusual to set men to work with shovel and pickaxe to fill up ruts and holes in roads seldom used by carriages, on such special occasions as a funeral or a wedding.'

Clearly the Austen family with its farm would need to be self-sufficient. In her letters written later in life Jane Austen often describes the poor condition of the lane from the rectory. For the growing child there must have been times when the small village seemed very remote; indeed by contrast trips into Basingstoke must have been great events. Even with modern transport the village retains its remoteness, a quiet that one imagines in 1771 could be as oppressive as it was peaceful.

The church of St Nicholas at Steventon is tiny. Set far up a lane well away from the road it is little altered since George Austen's day. The thirteenth-century building, so small that one imagines that the Austen family would fill it if they all attended church together, stands among trees at the edge of fields. A small spire has been added to the church since Jane Austen knew it, but the yew tree by the porch remains. The few graves in the churchyard bear witness to the smallness of the parish and indicate the nature of Jane's father's duties. This was no bustling parish with the need for many curates to help with services. The Rev George Austen's work would be in the village and among the scattered cottages. So small a community would necessarily be close-knit bordering upon other similar small communities. The rural setting and the remoteness of the village, while ensuring a certain isolation, would lead to the necessity for journeying, to sallying forth into the world. It is little wonder that visiting and letter-writing should be so important in Jane Austen's life. George Austen kept a carriage and, ruts or no ruts in the lane, his family took an active part in the social life of the area. These excursions from the rectory in the small hamlet out into the world and back again, when the weather permitted, might present a conducive experience for a young would-be story-teller.

The landscape of Steventon seems peculiarly familiar to those who know Jane Austen's writings well. Her nephew's description of its charms may be said in some ways also to outline the scope of her novels:

Jane Austen's mother, Cassandra Austen. Jane Austen's House, Chawton.

Jane Austen's father, 'the handsome proctor': a scholar of St John's College, Oxford, a school teacher and a parson. Jane Austen's House, Chawton.

*A pencil drawing by Anna Lefroy of the back of
Steventon Rectory. Jane Austen's House, Chawton.*

*A drawing by Anna Lefroy, one of Jane's favourite
nieces, of the front approach to Steventon Rectory,
Jane Austen's birthplace. It is now destroyed. Jane
Austen's House, Chawton.*

18

St Nicholas' Church, Steventon, from a photograph taken in 1860 with the 'spire' washed-out in order to show the church as Jane Austen would have known it. Her father was rector there from 1761 until 1801 . . Jane Austen's House, Chawton.

'. . . it presents no grand or extensive views; but the features are small rather than plain. The surface continually swells and sinks, but the hills are not bold, nor the valleys deep; and though it is sufficiently well clothed with woods and hedgerows, yet the poverty of the soil in some places prevents the timber from attaining a large size. Still it has its beauties. The lanes wind along in a natural curve, continually fringed with irregular borders of native turf and lead to pleasant nooks and corners.'

'No grand or extensive views' may well be translated into 'no great dramatic events', and the special 'small beauty' of the countryside may well with its hidden delights suggest to us the intricate subtleties of Jane Austen's own creations. Austen Leigh's account of Steventon concludes that its chief beauty lay in its hedgerows, his description of which aptly suggests the delight that the growing child could find in such a setting:

'A hedgerow, in that country, does not mean a thin formal line of quickset, but an irregular border of copse-wood and timber, often wide enough to contain within it a winding footpath, or a rough cart track. Under its shelter the earliest primroses, anemones, and wild hyacinths were to be found, sometimes, the first bird's nest; and now and then, the unwelcome adder. Two such hedgerows radiated, as it were, from the parsonage garden. One a continuation of the turf terrace, proceeded westward, forming the southern boundary of the home meadows; and was formed into a rustic shrubbery, with occasional seats, entitled 'the Wood Walk'.'

The Rectory itself was pulled down in 1826, but was improved and altered by George Austen to accommodate his large family and the pupils that he took in to add to his stipend. Originally little more than a cottage it was developed without pretension in a homely rather than a grand manner. Edward Austen Leigh considered the house unworthy and was critical of many of its features:

'. . . the rooms were finished with less elegance than would now be found in the most ordinary dwellings. No cornice marked the junction of wall and ceiling; while the beams which supported the upper floors projected into the rooms below in all their naked simplicity, covered only by a coat of paint or whitewash.'

But Jane's niece, Anna Lefroy, has left us a sketch of the Old Rectory, together with a written account of its interior:

'The dining- or common sitting-room looked to the front and was lighted by two casement windows. On the same side the front door opened into a smaller parlour, and visitors, who were few and rare, were not a bit the less welcome to my grandmother because they found her sitting there busily engaged with her needle, making and mending. In later times . . . a sitting-room was made upstairs: 'the dressing-room', as they were pleased to call it, perhaps because it opened into a smaller chamber in which my two aunts slept. I remember the common-looking carpet with its chocolate ground, and painted press with shelves above for books, and Jane's piano, and an oval looking glass that hung between the windows.'

Grand or homely, it was not the building that made the Austen rectory the home that it clearly was for Jane and for the other children who grew up there. Over the years, in the letters and memoirs, we hear of amateur dramatics in the barn, of charades, readings and music in the house. Outdoors Jane's older brothers hunted and shot game, while her mother managed a small herd of cows and a dairy. The world of Steventon Rectory seems to have been an attractive one. There is a story that on hearing that they were to leave the house and to go to live in Bath, Jane reacted in a way that she so despised romantic heroines for: she fainted. Clearly the years spent at Steventon were happy; they were the foundation for happy relationships within the family, between brothers and sisters, relationships which, judging from the warmth of the surviving letter, were to stand the test of time. The Austens of Steventon were a loving family who were not afraid to show or receive affection, affection, moreover, that was extended to in-laws and friends as readily as to Austens.

Of the pupils who lived and learnt with George Austen and his family we know little. Some time before Jane was born Warren Hastings' son came to live with her mother and father at the early age of three. Sadly he died of what was then called 'a putrid sore throat' (probably diphtheria) and it is said that Mrs Austen grieved as much as she would for her own child. In 1773 the eldest son of Lord Portsmouth came to live at the Rectory, a connection that was in time to ensure that the Austen young ladies, Jane and Cassandra, would have invitations to balls at Hurstbourne, the seat of the Portsmouths.

With an income of between £500 and £600 together with the money he could earn from teaching George Austen ministered in the parish of Steventon and Deane for thirty-seven years. That he was a good teacher is abundantly clear. He was to see his two sons, James and Henry, whom he had himself taught, go to his old college at Oxford. Both were eventually ordained, James succeeding his father as rector of Steventon.

Jane Austen spent the first twenty-five years of her life at Steventon, having, by the time that she left, completed early versions of three of the novels that she was later to rewrite and publish. Steventon played an important part in her development. It has often been said that she was never happy outside Hampshire. Some would claim that she was never really happy after leaving the Rectory at Steventon. Even today, the countryside around the church of St Nicholas and the walks through the fields and lanes around the villages that Jane Austen knew convey as much of her sense of place as the Haworth moors do of Emily Brontë. Ironically, life in Steventon Rectory was probably at times more remote and isolated than ever it was at Haworth Parsonage in the midst of the busy woollen industry.

We know little of Jane Austen's early life, apart from the fact that she was called 'Jenny' at home, and that she and her sister Cassandra, her senior by almost three years, became inseparable and were to remain lifelong confidantes and the most affectionate of sisters. It was through her devotion to Cassandra that Jane found herself leaving Steventon at the early age of six to set off for school in Oxford. As her mother commented, 'If Cassandra were going to have her head cut off, Jane would insist on sharing her fate'.

Childhood

'To scramble themselves into a little education'

WHILE young gentlemen came to George Austen's Rectory to be educated, his daughters Jane and Cassandra were sent away to begin theirs. It may be hard for us to see the logic of this exchange, but it was not an uncommon practice. Foreign observers of the British at home frequently noted the practice of 'putting one's children out' for their education. It came to be seen, along with the severity of punishments meted out in school and in the armed services, as 'the English way', as some kind of toughening-up process intended to enable the child to stand on his own feet. Whatever George Austen's reason, some suggest that it was to make room for the boarding boys who were a means of income, Cassandra and Jane set off for Oxford in 1782.

They were not going to strangers. Mrs Cawley, the widow of a Principal of Brasenose College who ran the school, was an 'in-law' relation of Jane's mother. The two little girls joined their cousin Jane Cooper, the headmistress's niece, in this first venture into the outside world. As it happened there was to be a tragedy, and one that came close to denying English literature its most renowned daughter. After a short time at Oxford the school removed lock stock and barrel to Southampton where that scourge of all such eighteenth-century establishments, 'the putrid sore throat', claimed the girls as serious victims. In a situation that was to be echoed when the two older Brontë children were found to be ill at Cowan Bridge School, the headmistress failed to inform the parents of the children's sickness. It was only when Jane Cooper had the sense to write to her mother at a time when Jane Austen was severely ill that the alarm was raised. With the haste that Patrick Brontë displayed some forty years later when he learnt of the illness of his elder children, the anxious mothers set off for Southampton. Fortunately Jane Austen recovered. Jane Cooper's mother, however, caught the infection from her daughter and died.

After a short time at Steventon another school, nearer to home, was found and once again Cassandra and Jane set off. This time it was to the Abbey School at Reading which was run by a Mrs Latournelle, by all accounts a lively and jovial lady who sported a cork artificial leg. Reports suggest that the school was very well run, which does not mean that its academic standards were high. In those days little education was thought necessary or advisable for girls. Contemporaries of Jane and Cassandra describe the school as a happy one where the girls had plenty of time to themselves. Set in part of Reading Abbey Gatehouse with its own garden Mrs Latournelle's establishment provided a much more healthy environment for young girls.

It is in many cases wrong to accept Jane Austen's fictitious descriptions and to apply them to real places and people. Her fiction is not her autobiography. However there might be something of Mrs Latournelle's school that would be held in common with those establishments described by Jane Austen in *Emma*:
'. . . a real, honest, old-fashioned boarding-school, where a reasonable quantity of accomplishments were sold at a reasonable price, and where girls might be sent to be out of the way and scramble themselves into a little education, without any danger of coming back prodigies.' [Vol. I, Chapter III]
Cassandra and Jane stayed with Mrs Latournelle, who reputedly talked more about actors and plays than about any other subject, from 1785 until the spring of 1787. Nothing is known of the curriculum followed or of any 'accomplishments' that Jane might have developed at Reading. It is commonly believed that her real education began on her return home to Steventon on her readmission into the stimulating and learned environment that her father and considerably older brothers created and maintained. Writing in 1801 before the move to Bath Jane tells us that in selling up

the Rectory, her father had 'above 500 volumes to dispose of'. George Austen had collected a fine library in his years as rector. It is 'above 500 volumes' that young writers need to secure their own particular as well as ordinary education. Henry Austen's brief biographical note to his young sister's posthumously published *Northanger Abbey* and *Persuasion*, supports the view that a better education was to be had at Steventon than in many a 'real, honest, old-fashioned boarding school'. Of his father George, he comments:

'Being not only a profound scholar, but possessing a most exquisite taste in every species of literature, it is not wonderful that his daughter Jane should at a very early age become sensible to the charms of style and enthusiastic in the cultivation of her own language.'

'The cultivation of her own language' is precisely what Jane Austen set about. Words were to her playthings in her own personal life, and in her writing for publication she developed a sensitivity and confidence that resulted in a fine facility with English prose. It was the society which she found in her home that provoked the enthusiasm for and exploration of styles and techniques that were to become so eloquent a vehicle for her ideas.

'THE AUSTENS AT HOME'

Jane Austen's return to her family was a return to those whom she loved and whose company she cherished. She was interested and involved in family matters above all else. Most of her life was spent dealing with three generations of her family as daughter, sister and aunt. If we are to know her we must somehow get to know her family. This is, however, no straightforward matter, as R.W. Chapman, the most celebrated authority on the Austen family, pointed out in the Clark Lectures, Cambridge 1948:

'The task is not easy; for the Austens and their relations by marriage were numerous and prolific; and their historian, labouring to be lucid, is embarrassed by their tendency to marry twice, and to change and amplify their surnames.'

When we consider that five of Jane's brothers married nine wives and that they all had large families, we can appreciate the problem. To the family proper must be added the very large circles of acquaintances and in-laws who formed part of the Austens' social circle.

All the evidence from letters and memoirs indicates that the members of the family enjoyed a good-humoured and close relationship with one another. This is certainly true from the evidence in Jane's own surviving letters which we shall consider in detail in a later chapter. The list of relatives and friends to whom and about whom letters were written is formidable. Clearly the Rectory was a busy household during the period that the young Jane was growing up.

A recipe for 'Pease Soup' by Martha Lloyd, who stayed with Jane for many years. Housekeeping was as much a feature of life at the Rectory as was literary discussion.

The Abbey Gateway, Reading, from a painting by Paul Sandby. The Abbey school at Reading which Jane attended in the 1780s used a part of this building. Victoria and Albert Museum, London.

By 1787 Jane's older brothers were already away from home. There was a ten year difference in age between her and her eldest brother James, who, having achieved a degree at his father's old college at fourteen, was now a fellow. Without doubt the first-born son was the scholar of the family. While at Oxford he edited a journal, *The Loiterer*, which was proof of his interest in writing and literature. This interest seems everywhere in the Austen household, for when Henry joined his brother James at Oxford, he too was to write for *The Loiterer*, a journal which, as its title might indicate, was aimed at university men, being '. . . a rough but not entirely inaccurate Sketch of the Character, the manners and Amusements of Oxford at the close of the century.'

The literary aspirations of Jane's brothers provide another example of the stimulating household of which George Austen, himself an acknowledged scholar, was the head. Unlike their fellow undergraduates, who were renowned for their gambling, hunting, wild living and disregard for scholarship, the Austen brothers seemed to have enjoyed the university for its concern with literature and academic studies as much as for its social life.

Henry Austen, three years older than Jane, is clearly her favourite older brother. While following his brother James to his father's old college—he left for Oxford the year after Jane and Cassandra returned from the Reading school—he seems to have combined the qualities of scholar with those of a 'loiterer'. Henry Austen's was a colourful and eventful career that spanned the Oxford Militia, Banking—he became receiver general for Oxfordshire then a bankrupt—and eventually the Church.

James's daughter Anna gives us a description of her Uncle Henry, who with his father's hazel eyes, and with his gaiety and good humour seems to have been thoroughly likeable:

'He was the handsomest of the family, and in the opinion of his father, the most talented. There were others who formed a different opinion, but, for the most part, he was greatly admired. Brilliant in conversation he was, and, like his father, blessed with a hopefulness of temper which in adapting itself to all circumstances, served to create a perpetual sunshine.'

While it is believed that James encouraged Jane's critical response to literature, it was the less stable and

*A very fine example of the popular art of the
silhouette, here showing the presentation by George
Austen of his son Edward to Mr and Mrs Thomas
Knight for adoption. It is perhaps a shock for us to
realize that Jane's father wore a wig, frock-coat and
silk-stockings. Major Edward Knight, Chawton
House.*

more colourful Henry who was to help her more
effectively in her writing and literary career. It was he
who dealt with her publishers on her behalf, though
with characteristic hubris, it was also he who betrayed
the secret of her authorship against her wishes. Predictably Jane was to forgive him.

Writing of his early preaching and of his fortitude at
the death of his first wife, Jane indicates something of the
respect and affection which she showed him:

> Our own new clergyman is expected here very
> soon, perhaps in time to assist Mr Papillon on
> Sunday. I shall be very glad when the first
> hearing is over. It will be a nervous hour in our
> pew, though we hear that he acquits himself
> with as much ease and collectedness, as if he
> had been used to it all his life.
> [Letter to Alethea Bigg, 24 January 1817]

At the death of Eliza, Henry's wife, Jane writes:

> We are in hopes of another visit from our own
> true, lawful Henry very soon . . . Upon the
> whole his Spirits are very much recovered. – If

I may so express myself, his Mind is not the
Mind for affliction. He is too busy, too active,
too sanguine, – sincerely as he was attached to
Eliza moreover, and excellently as he behaved
to her, he was always so used to be away from
her at times, that her Loss is not felt as that of
many a beloved wife might be, especially
when all the circumstances of her long and
dreadful illness are taken into the account.
(Letter to Francis Austen, 3 July 1813)

When during her last illness Jane was being taken to
Winchester, where she was to die, it was Henry who
rode on horseback in the pouring rain accompanying
the coach that carried his sister.

Henry's spirit was almost matched by that of his
brother Frank who was only one year older than Jane.
Frank more than the others has left us a vivid image of
the outward-looking and cheerful life that was at times
possible in the rectory. From an early age all the Austen
boys hunted: Steventon lies in the heart of the Vine
hunt, a prime hunting area. There persisted a story in
the Austen family of Frank buying a pony called
Squirrel for a guinea when he was seven years old,
making it jump over everything that it could see over,
and then finally re-selling it for a guinea more than he
had paid.

Charles Austen, the baby of the family, was always
the object of special affection by the two girls, Cassandra

24

and Jane. For he was their own 'special' little brother.

Frank and Charles were both to leave home to attend the Royal Naval Academy at Portsmouth. Both had very successful careers in the navy, ending their service as admirals.

Jane's sister Cassandra was, above all other members of the family, her closest companion and soul-mate. She was the 'Miss Austen' of the family, the title 'Miss Austen' going to the eldest daughter according to the custom of the day. Should Cassandra have married, then, and only then, would Jane be called Miss Austen. But as this was not to be, our subject was always known to the world as 'Miss *Jane* Austen', the use of her Christian name indicating that she was the second daughter of the family. Jane readily accepted her subordinate role, jokingly referring to herself as 't'other Miss Austen'. Jane's admiration for her older sister never faltered and the story persists that she considered her taste, judgement and accomplishments in every way superior to her own. In a letter, Jane refers to Cassandra as 'the finest comic writer of the present age'. However seriously we might choose to take such a claim, it indicates a generosity towards Cassandra that is maintained throughout the sisters' correspondence. Cassandra and Jane lived together with their mother

Jane Austen's only sister Cassandra, to whom many of the surviving letters were written. She outlived her sister by twenty-eight years.

Edward Austen (later Knight). A portrait painted when he was sent by his benefactor, Thomas Knight, on 'The Grand Tour'. Jane Austen's House, Chawton.

throughout Jane's life. It is not surprising, therefore, to find that in their letters, made necessary by the visits that they each in turn made to brothers, friends and other relatives, there is the most detailed sisterly gossip as well as the expected discussion of literature and business matters.

Of Jane's brothers, Edward, the third son of the family, provides the most intriguing story. Scholarly though James might be, handsome and delightful though the unpredictable Henry might be, it was Edward who was to provide the link with wealth and the more well-connected side of the Austen family. It would be uncharitable to suggest that this was not of his own doing and did not come as a result of his own exertions, but it is true that his career and fortunes were offered to him before he was of an age to seek them himself. It was his good fortune to be adopted into the wealthy family of a distant relative. Thomas Knight the elder had presented the Rev George Austen with a living, and now his son, another Thomas Knight, owner of most of the parish of Steventon, whose country seat was at Godmersham, offered to adopt the young Edward with a view to making him his heir. Thus the generosity of one generation found an echo in the next.

Thomas Knight and his wife Catherine were childless and, finding that they liked the good humoured Edward when they met him during a visit to Steventon, they

OF THE

LOITERER.

Speak of us as we are.

PRINTED FOR THE AUTHOR,

And fold by C. S. RANN, OXFORD; Meffrs. EGER-
TONS, Whitehall, LONDON; Meffrs. PEARSON and
ROLLASON, BIRMINGHAM; Mr. W. MEYLER,
Grove, BATH; and Meffrs. COWSLADE and SMART,
READING.

MDCCLXXXIX.

On the whole, therefore, fhould the Merit of thefe Pages be fufficient to recommend them to the occafional and curfory perufal of his Fellow Students, the Author of the LOITERER will reflect with pleafure on having added his Mite to the common ftock of Public Amufement. Should it even fail, he will not think the time beftowed on this work wholly thrown away, fince it has introduced him to the knowledge of men, on whofe acquaintance he reflects at once with pride and pleafure, and fince it has filled up many hours which might have been loft in vacant indolence, or engroffed by lefs innocent occupations.

JAMES AUSTEN, M.A.

St. JOHN's COLLEGE,
March 20th, 1790.

C.

F I N I S.

⁎ Thofe Subfcribers who wifh to collect thefe Effays into volumes, may be furnifhed in the courfe of a few weeks with *a Table of Contents, Errata,* &c. by applying to Meff. PRINCE and COOKE; of whom may be had, compleat Sets, or fingle Numbers.

Sample pages of The Loiterer, *a university magazine which Jane's elder brothers James and Henry edited for a long while. They are evidence of the literary atmosphere in which she was reared. Jane was fifteen when this edition was published. The Library, St John's College, Oxford.*

---

prevailed upon his father and mother to let him come to live with them. The tradition is that George Austen feared for the boy lest he neglect his lessons, and that it was his wife's 'I think, my dear, you had better oblige your cousins and let the child go', that gained his consent. Thus Edward Austen went to live in a great house from which he so 'obliged his father's cousins' that he inherited the whole of the estate of Thomas Knight which included Chawton Manor among its various assets. Edward's adoption, a not untypical occurrence in families seeking to perpetuate their ownership through kin wherever possible, not only made his fortune but removed the urgency of financial worries from the entire Austen household as the years passed. Edward clearly played his part well and grew to repay the faith that his benefactors had bestowed in him. At Thomas Knight's death, his widow resigned her property in Edward's favour and he changed his name to Knight accordingly.

Edward's translation into the 'real' gentry was to benefit the Austen family in many ways, as we shall see. Most important of all must have been the security that it gave them, which was especially clearly seen on the occasion of the Rev George Austen's death when the widow and daughters were left to fend for themselves. Edward, then as in so many cases, was in a position to help, both with money, and eventually with the provision of a house on one of his own estates. The importance of such security in the eighteenth century is incalculable. At another level Edward's life style and his circle of acquaintances, indeed his own marriage, was to bring the Austen family into contact with people that they would not otherwise have met as equals. This latter possibility is of prime significance when we consider the society that Jane Austen recreates and of which she displays so detailed a knowledge in her novels.

Edward must have proved a good *son* to the Knights who in turn provided him with the upbringing that would ensure his success as a landlord and manager of large estates. For Edward it was the grand tour, on which Thomas Knight sent him, that was to prepare him for a career where he had to be able to manage men and money. The ability to organize oneself travelling through Europe could be as helpful an education as 'loitering' in the cloisters of colleges for a man with Edward's prospects.

Edward had already left for Godmersham when Jane and Cassandra returned from their Reading schooldays. It is known, however, that visits were frequent and that Edward was by no means lost to the family forever. Godmersham and Edward's life there features frequently in the story of the Austens, not the least in Jane's comings and goings.

The Austen family was a lively one. What we know of Jane's early years gives an impression of bustle and activity with the opportunity for much shared pleasure. All commentators note the sense of happiness that is to be found in the memoirs and accounts of Steventon in the middle of the century. Life could not, however, have been all one round of delights. Jane herself records the appalling state of the lanes and the difficulty in getting about even in pattens. It is easy to forget many of the hardships that were commonplace in the 1700s, the lack of real medical knowledge, the poor sanitation, and the dependence upon a good harvest. Similarly we should not forget that we are concerned with Georgian England which for all its sometime elegance was in no way a fastidious age. Life in the Rectory farmhouse would be bracing and vigorous, for Jane Austen lived long before the Victorian ideal of the pale delicate young lady with an exquisite distaste for practical matters. Life in Georgian Steventon could be very un-ladylike and we know from her letters that Jane Austen did not flinch from practical problems or occurrences. A lady who can announce in a letter that 'tomorrow we are to kill a pig!' is, for all her poise and good manners, also the lady who can bake bread, brew beer and tease her young niece

about fleas in her bed.

The life of the family was robust and eventful. The enterprise of her brothers and their zeal for the outdoor life complemented their father's scholarly ways. It is tempting to conclude that life for a growing child in the rectory was in all probability a very balanced one, and a synthesis of influences of various kinds. In the later Austen family it was believed that Jane was a blend of both her parents' natures:

'If one may divide qualities which often overlap, one would be inclined to surmise that Jane Austen inherited from her father her serenity of mind, the refinement of her intellect, and her delicate appreciation of style, while her mother supplied the acute observation of character, and the wit and humour, for which she was equally distinguished.'

Jane's mother had an interest in farming, and in June 1773 she is known to have had 'a nice dairy fitted up' consisting of 'a bull and six cows' as stock. This would offer the growing Jane a splendid contrast to the delicacies of style in literature. Throughout her letters there are many references to animals, often in quite practical and unsentimental terms, and we read of sheep, pigs, turkeys, ducks, chickens and bee-keeping.

Life at the Rectory need not have been dull, but because of its situation in the depths of the countryside it would necessarily be the life of a closely-knit group. The varied interests and careers of the family would bring a constant flow of information and talk about all kinds of subjects. The Rectory/farmhouse would be a stimulating and at times bustling place offering a very full experience for growing children of sound limb and quick imagination.

Commending a careful study of Jane's letters, R.W. Chapman rightly suggests that the study of the Austen family is a rewarding one in its own right:

'The family and its connexions are attractive in themselves—a vigorous, versatile race—and the social scene which their lives make up is drawn by our observer (Jane Austen) with rare delicacy and skill. The social historian has at his command no equal picture of the life of the upper middle class in England in George the Third's last years.' [Clark Lectures, Cambridge 1948]

World Events Impinge

IN THE YEAR 1787 world events came to the door of George Austen's rectory at Steventon. It was in the next decade to become the scene for sadness and personal grief caused directly by events in France. Jane's home, during the years that cover the writing of her first recorded and surviving stories, was sensitive to affairs abroad because relatives and people living there were directly and personally involved. For Jane Austen the reign of terror in France that marked the French Revolution after the execution of Louis XVI was to be a lasting shock and a personal distress.

It was in 1787 that George Austen's niece came to stay at Steventon. The only daughter of his sister Philadelphia, Eliza, already married, rather grandly to a French aristocrat, brought her baby boy and a great deal of excitement and gaiety to the Austen family. Eliza, after finishing her education in Paris, had married the Comte de Feuillide, and had found that being a 'Comtesse' well suited her temperament and high spirits. Through her father and mother's connection with Warren Hastings, who was her godfather and in whose honour her son was christened Hastings, she had money of her own as well as the position that her marriage ensured. Fifteen years older than Jane, Eliza, Comtesse de Feuillide, with her assurance and accomplishments, would be a heady companion for a young woman and an intriguing study for an observant young writer.

Eliza, perhaps predictably, adored acting. Her stay in 1787 saw a revival of the family amateur dramatics that took place in the large barn across the lane.

Reading aloud, story-telling and acting their own compositions as well as written plays was all part of the Austen family tradition. A farm barn was used from time to time which had already seen a production of *The Rivals*, and it appears that Eliza was the cause of yet more productions. It is generally believed that she took

leading roles—the tone of her letters would suggest this—and it seems certain that among her male cousins her charms would not be overlooked. The twelve-year-old Jane would have her own view of the excitement that accompanied the rehearsing and performing of Garrick's *Bon Ton* and Mrs Cowley's *Which is the Man*. Later, in *Mansfield Park*, Jane was to draw upon the experiences she witnessed and show her intimate knowledge of the particular pleasures and difficulties that accompany amateur dramatics.

Throughout the years that followed, Eliza and her mother feature frequently in Steventon affairs. The baby Hastings, born in 1786, was very much the plaything of the family. It had been some time since there had been a baby at the Rectory and the young boy was the first of the next generation to appear.

It is another cousin of Jane's who tells us not only of Eliza but gives us one of the first accounts of Jane as a person. Of the Comtesse, Jane's cousin Philadelphia Walter, who for some reason would not take part in the Steventon dramatics, comments:

'The Countess has many amiable qualities, such as the highest duty, love, and respect for her mother: for whom there is not any sacrifice she would not make, and certainly contributes entirely to her happiness: for her husband she professes a large share of respect, esteem and the highest opinion of his merits, but confesses that love is not of the number on her side, tho' still very violent on his: her principles are strictly just, making it a rule never to bespeak anything she is not quite sure of being able to pay for directly, never contracting debts of any kind. Her dissipated life she was brought up to—therefore it cannot be wondered at, but her religion is not changed.'

Philadelphia's rather harsh judgement of her cousin, who in fairness saw herself at times as 'the greatest rake imaginable' being out till 'five in the morning' at

Eliza de la Feuillide, Jane's rather giddy cousin. Eliza eventually married Henry Austen, although it is said that Mrs. Austen disapproved of the alliance.

The trial of Warren Hastings in Westminster Hall. The Austen family followed Hastings' lengthy trial with interest, having family connections with him.

Almacks, may set the scene for her rather peevish view of her other cousin, Jane Austen:

'As it's pure Nature to love ourselves I may be allowed to give preference to the Eldest who is generally reckoned a most striking resemblance to me in features, complexion and manners . . . the youngest [Jane] is very like her brother Henry, not at all pretty and very prim, unlike a girl of twelve: but it is hasty judgement which you will scold me for . . .

. . . I continue to admire my amiable likeness the best of the two in every respect: she keeps up conversation in a very sensible and pleasing manner. Yesterday they all spent the day with us, and the more I see of Cassandra the more I admire her – Jane is whimsical and affected.' Before returning to France Eliza paid her cousins at St. John's, Oxford, a visit, and once again it is through her that we have a glimpse of the family:

'My cousin James met us there, and as well as his brother [Henry] was so good as to take the trouble of showing us the lions. We visited several of the colleges, the museum etc and were very elegantly entertained by our gallant relations at St. John's . . . I do not think you would know Henry with his hair powdered and dressed in a very *tonish* style, besides he is at present taller than his father.'

By the Christmas of 1788 Eliza had returned to France and the plays in the barn had to go on without her. There now begins one of the busiest times for the Austen family where changes come thick and fast.

The Fall of the Bastille: an event which had far-reaching implications for Jane and her family.

Already Jane was busy writing; her earliest recorded and surviving pieces date from these years. It is not surprising to find that among them there are pieces dedicated to Eliza, pieces, moreover, that in their theme and style suit the character of the gay energetic Comtesse:

Love and Friendship
a novel
in a series of letters.
'Deceived in Friendship and Betrayed in Love'
To Madame La Comtesse
De Feuillide This Novel is Inscribed
by Her obliged Humble Servant The Author

Together with her connection with French aristocracy Eliza provided yet another link between Steventon and the affairs of the world beyond Hampshire. In the same year that she came to her cousins to tread their barn-theatre-boards, her godfather, Warren Hastings, was put on trial for impeachment. The trial was very much a showpiece, its course and its outcome interesting many besides the Austen family who held a very partisan view of its proceedings. The trial in Westminster Hall was to drag on for eight years ending with

Hastings' acquittal. It is worth contrasting his fate as victim of a public spectacle with that of many in similar situations in France.

Hastings' trial covers the period of the reign of terror that overtook France when the 'citizens' arraigned the aristocracy before themselves for judgement. Haydn was among the foreign visitors who attended sessions of Warren Hastings' trial astonished by the spectacle of a man of wealth and standing having to face trial by the Commons. Revolution was in the air and such show trials bred more than a slight unease. The year that the trial ended saw George III's coach attacked by a mob and the slogans 'No King–No Parliament' daubed on the walls of the streets of London.

It did not rest with the outside world to bring news of these affairs to the Austen family. When Eliza brought the young Hastings to be pampered by her cousins, Frank had already left home to undergo his training in the Royal Navy. Frank was away in the East Indies for four years, and returned as a lieutenant just one year after his brother Charles, the youngest of the Austen boys, was to enter the Royal Naval Academy at Portsmouth to begin his naval career. For fifty-seven years of Frank's life and forty-six of Charles's, Jane Austen's brothers were actively engaged in maintaining British supremacy at sea. For the whole of the rest of her life Jane knew what it was to have brothers taking part in the actions which were to be constantly reported in the newspapers. Their combined service covered every aspect of the country's wars and Jane's letters chronicle her brothers' whereabouts and activities throughout her life. Her father's letter to Frank when he sailed on his first ship, the *Perseverance*, at fourteen, indicates both the concern of the father and something of the strong family ties that the Austens valued:

> I have nothing to add but my blessing and best prayers for your health and prosperity, and to beg you would never forget you have not upon earth a more disinterested and warm friend than your truly affectionate father.

ROMANCE

The years between December 1786 and December 1796 when she was twenty-one saw many changes both in Jane's family and in her own interests and abilities. In 1786 she was busy with her early writings enjoying the comparatively undisciplined frolicking with words that all young writers indulge in. By 1796 she was writing more sustained pieces which her father was prepared the following year to offer to a London publisher.

The development in Jane's writing is rapid, indicating a growing confidence that must have come from wide reading and lively discussion. The developments in the family circumstances would offer ready material for an observant chronicler and many opportunities for kindly parody and pastiche. Marriage was in the air. The growing young woman could observe her older brothers' romances and their subsequent marriages. With Eliza de Feuillide's high sense of 'courtship' at large in the Rectory Jane could take the ready-made theme of 'falling in love' and explore its hilarious as well as its practical implications in the style of the popular fiction of the day. The young Jane was a satirist, and it was the absurdities of swooning lovers and the inelegances of passion that she delighted to depict in her early explorations with words.

Edward, by now confidently established with the Knight family, was the first of the brothers to marry. At twenty-one he made a match in keeping with his

---

In February 1794, the husband of Jane's cousin Eliza was guillotined. It is said that from that day the name of France made Jane Austen shudder. Eliza stayed with Jane's family at the time of her husband's execution.

George III reviewing his troops before they departed to engage Napoleon. The Prince of Wales is at his side and strikes a pose with a cavalry sabre. (Painted for George III, 1797-98.) Royal Collection.

elevation into landed gentry, marrying Elizabeth Bridges, the daughter of Sir Brooke Bridges who was a man of property as well as title. It is to Edward's credit that his moving into such elevated circles did not divorce him from his own family. The Knights and the Austens always remained on good terms with frequent visiting taking place, particularly from Cassandra. As ever with George Austen's family any marriage seemed to extend it and enlarge the company of acquaintances rather than diminish the affection and close bonds that existed.

The year after Edward's marriage in 1791, his elder brother James, now curate at Overton, married Anne Mathew. Again it was a 'good' match, her parents being General Mathew and Lady Jane, the daughter of the second Duke of Ancaster.

There was yet a third romance and marriage from the rectory in 1792. Jane Cooper, Jane Austen's school-friend cousin, married a Captain Williams of the Royal Navy, and, as both her parents were dead, it was from the rectory that she left Steventon on her wedding day.

It was into this world with so much news of weddings and changes in circumstances that Eliza returned from France. Her son's health was not good, and with her mother also ill she returned to Margate, where it was hoped the sea air would benefit the invalids. Her husband accompanied her, taking her to Bath after her mother's death early in 1792. Things in France were going from bad to worse and soon the Comte de Feuillide was summoned back. It was not a good time to be an aristocrat and he was warned that if he did not return he would be deemed to have emigrated and would forfeit his property. With her husband's return to France and its attendant anxieties Eliza, whose spirits were uncharacteristically low, decided to spend the rest of the summer at Steventon where she hoped that 'the quiet and good air will be of great service to my health which indeed stands much in need of some such restorative'. The peace and companionship of the Austen family proved a great attraction. Jane was by this time sixteen and by all accounts a handsome young woman, being very slender with brown curly hair. Eliza found both Austen girls much improved:

> Cassandra and Jane are both very much grown (the latter is now taller than myself) and greatly improved as well in manners as in person, both of which are now much more formed than they were when you saw them. They are, I think, equally sensible, and both so to a degree seldom met with, but still my heart gives preference to Jane, whose kind partiality to me indeed requires a return of the same nature.

The year 1792 saw the further deterioration of things in France with the country being declared a republic and a revolutionary tribunal being set up. The news coming to Steventon became less and less reassuring. England watched the situation with great concern. Some, like the young Wordsworth, hailed the new age as one of freedom and liberation, while others were deeply troubled by the whiff of rebellion that drifted across the English Channel. It would not be long before the Duke of Gloucester, the king's brother, was to stalk out of a concert of music at York House because he had 'spotted' (erroneously as it turned out) 'a *Frenchman* playing the double bass'.

In 1793, the Revolution reached a climax with the execution of Louis XVI. England, horrified at this crime against a monarch, declared war on France. George III reviewed his troops, and the *London Times* set out, on 8 February 1793, the reasons for beginning a war that was to last for many more years than anyone could have foreseen:

'The public mind is now wholly occupied by the great and important question of WAR; and the justification of its NECESSITY is the subject of our present consideration.

We are free to confess, that a war with FRANCE appears to us not only to be founded on the strict rules of retaliation, but also of self-defence against *principles* which tend to disorganize every existing government, and to destroy all social order. There is not a power in Europe but possesses one common interest to stop the progress of the new political French disease; and the people are equally bound to secure themselves from this pestilential contagion, which for four years past has desolated the finest kingdom in the universe. The approaching war is entered on with reluctance. It is not, as was formerly the case, a war between ambitious Kings who sacrificed millions of men to ascertain the right of an insignificant town or province; it is not even a war of one nation against another, dictated by commercial interests; but it is a coalition of all regular and well established governments, and of every civilized people, against a system of anarchy, deliberative in its principles, and disastrous in its consequences . . .'

Few realized in February 1793 that the young officers setting out for the first 'modern war' would be in their forties before it was over in 1815.

It was the following year, 1794, when Jane was eighteen that the Austen family knew at first hand the effects of the 'new political French disease'. In France the 'reign of terror' had begun, the Committee of Public Safety had commenced its bizarre proceedings, and Eliza's husband found himself in their clutches. His friend the Marquise de Marlboef had been accused of deliberately setting out to cause a famine, merely because some of her land was used for growing hay for her cattle rather than corn for people. With ill-advised goodwill the Comte de Feuillide gallantly sought to defend his friend. Foolishly he attempted to bribe witnesses, was arrested, tried and guillotined on the same day as the marquise whom he had sought to help. The distant horrors of Paris, the 'war that was safely in the newspapers', came tragically and horrifically into Steventon Rectory. It is said that Jane Austen could never think of France without a shudder after the news of Eliza's husband's execution. For whatever reason she chose not to put the Napoleonic wars into her novels it cannot be because she did not know about them. The war with France was perhaps of greater significance in the Austen household than in many others. After all, Eliza was married to a Frenchman, and her personal maid Madame Bigeon, who lived with her in the Rectory, was also one of the Duke of Gloucester's dreaded French.

1795 saw the finish of the Warren Hastings trial, both Jane's brothers at sea in the Royal Navy that was at war, and was to end with the first tragedy in the more direct family circle. James's wife, Anne, died leaving a very young daughter, Anna. The child came to the Rectory to live and was brought up by her sister-aunts Jane and Cassandra. So the tragic and changeful decade was to close on a note of promise. While herself maturing in her writing and her personal life, Jane was to take a significant part in the nurture of one of her first nieces. She was to prove as good an aunt as we know her to be a writer.

Jane:

'cheerfulness, sensibility, and benevolence'

J. Austen

IT IS IMPOSSIBLE for us ever to know completely with any confidence what Jane Austen was really like. With the distortions of our imaginations and the scarcity of any objective description we can but guess. The very first conscious attempt to introduce her to a larger circle than her own family came from Henry Austen, the brother who helped her manage her publishing affairs. After her death in 1817 he added the *Biographical Notice of the Author* to the posthumous edition of *Northanger Abbey* and *Persuasion*. As we might expect from a brother and an eloquent clergyman this account is partial and favourable:

'Of personal attractions she possessed a considerable share. Her stature was that of true elegance. It could not have been increased without exceeding the middle height. Her carriage and deportment were quiet, yet graceful. Her features were separately good. Their assemblage produced an unrivalled expression of that cheerfulness, sensibility, and benevolence, which were her real characteristics.'

So writes a grieving brother about his younger novelist sister only one year after her death. But allowing for his partiality Henry does give us a view of the Jane that we all seek to know:

'Her complexion was of the finest texture. It might with truth be said, that her eloquent blood spoke through her modest cheek. Her voice was extremely sweet. She delivered herself with fluency and precision. Indeed she was formed for elegant and rational society, excelling in conversation as much as in composition.'

The epithets fit our picture of the author of *Emma* and *Pride and Prejudice*; we can through our own observance of her 'fluency and precision' in the novels readily believe that the sister possessed the qualities which she so deftly displays as novelist.

It is from another member of the family that we are given further details. Because his father James Austen was unwell it was the nine-year-old James E. Austen Leigh who represented Jane's eldest brother at her funeral. Almost fifty years after that day in Winchester he compiled a Memoir of his Aunt that remains, despite its 'partisan' nature, a charming and useful account:

'In person she was very attractive; her figure was rather tall and slender, her step light and firm, and her whole appearance expressive of health and animation. In complexion she was a clear brunette with a rich colour; she had full round cheeks, with mouth and nose small and well formed, light hazel eyes, and brown hair forming natural curls close round her face. If not so regularly handsome as her sister, yet her countenance had a peculiar charm of its own to the eyes of most beholders.'

To complete these sketches of the revered relative there is Henry's outline of Jane's accomplishments:

'Our authoress . . . had not only an excellent taste for drawing, but, in her earlier days, evinced great power of hand in the management of the pencil. Her own musical attainments she held very cheap. Twenty years ago they would have been thought more of, and twenty years hence many a parent will expect their daughters to be applauded for meaner performances. She was fond of dancing, and excelled in it.'

Fortunately there is other evidence besides these rather stiff, almost obligatory praises. From the tone as much as from the content of more personal family reminiscences we glimpse a human being of more convincing substance than this shadowy elegant paragon. One of Jane Austen's nieces confides in the Memoir:

'As a very little girl I was always creeping up to Aunt Jane and following her wherever I could in the house and out of it . . . she seemed to love you and you loved her in return.'

Another niece of more mature years adds:

'. . . as I grew older, when the original seventeen years between our ages seemed to shrink to seven or to nothing, it comes back to me now how strangely I missed her. It had become so much a habit with me to put by things in my mind with a reference to her, and to say to myself, I shall keep this for Aunt Jane.'

But perhaps the most telling testimonial comes from the nephew who was puzzled after her death:

'. . . his visits to Chawton, after the death of his Aunt Jane, were always a disappointment to him. From old associations he could not help expecting to be particularly happy in that house; and never till he got there could he realise to himself how all its peculiar charm was gone.'

From these and other such fragments we can compose a portrait of an elusive figure: the Aunt who was the respected confidante of young nieces in love, (the letters containing her gentle advice survive); the weaver of fairy tales; the conversationalist; the young woman of elegant carriage who excelled at dancing.

How much are we to believe of such charmed reporters?

There were other views. Mary Russell Mitford, in a notoriously irreverent mood, revelled in a fine piece of malice:

> I have discovered that our great favourite Miss Austen is my countrywoman; that Mama knew all her family very intimately; and that she herself is an old maid (I beg her pardon–I mean young lady) with whom Mama before her marriage was acquainted. Mama says she was then the prettiest, silliest, most affected husband-hunting butterfly she ever remembers and a friend of mine who visits her now says that she has stiffened into the most perpendicular, precise, taciturn piece of 'single blessedness' that ever existed, and that till 'Pride and Prejudice' showed what a precious gem was hidden in that unbending case, she was no more regarded in society than a poker or a fire screen or any other thin, upright piece of wood or iron that fills its corner in peace and quiet. The case is very different now; she is still a poker but a poker of whom everyone is afraid. It must be confessed that this silent observation from such an observer is rather formidable . . . a wit, a delineator of character who does not talk is formidable indeed.

[Letter to Sir William Elford, April 1815]

In our own century Sir Harold Nicolson, fulminating over his disappointment with Jane Austen's letters, permits himself the thought that she might not, after all, have been wholly pleasant to know:

'The reader 'settles down to enjoy himself', and

Tunes for dances which we know Jane Austen danced. She was an enthusiastic dancer and, according to her family and friends, a very good one. Jane Austen's House, Chawton.

once again comes over him that feeling of perplexed disappointment. It is not merely that Jane Austen's letters to her sister Cassandra are trivial and dull. It is far worse than that. Inevitably, as we plough through this desert of family gossip, this catalogue of sun-bonnets, the ghastly thought arises that Jane Austen had a mind like a very small, sharp pair of scissors, attached by a pink ribbon to a very neat and maidenly work-basket.' [*New Statesman and Nation*, 26 November 1932]

Fortunately, we are in a position to make our own judgement here. Readers like Nicolson are disappointed because they do not see the letters in the context in which they were written. But if we ourselves approach them in a less high-minded way, we–between the bonnets and the supposedly boring family gossip–may find Jane Austen's own voice in a natural confiding tone. The letters, which were written with an implicit faith that they would never be read by any other than the person to whom they were addressed and posted,

London head-dresses of around 1800. There is much talk of hats in Jane Austen's letters. Top centre in this illustration is the 'Mameluke cap' which became fashionable after Nelson's victory at the Battle of the Nile. Jane Austen's letters tell us that she wore such a cap at Lord Portsmouth's Ball. Victoria and Albert Museum, London.

offer us because of this intimacy perhaps the most secure description of the novelist and person. Sometimes she does indeed write of bonnets, what sister has not to another? Sometimes she will write of family gossip, that staple of all true drama, and sometimes she even writes of her own love of writing. If we are to pry into private letters it is for us to seek to meet the particular nature of the correspondence that it is our privilege to see. We should not presume, as E.M. Forster did, to say that Jane Austen was a bad letter writer, merely because she does not fill her pages with the eloquent explorations of her art as a novelist which we would perhaps like to read.

Whatever the disadvantages of meeting Jane Austen through her private correspondence, it is in her letters that we can most clearly detect her personality. Some, however, would wish to see such an exploration denied. The poet Tennyson, an admirer, who according to his son 'would read and re-read' Miss Austen's novels, '. . . thanked God Almighty with his whole heart that he knew nothing, and that the world knew nothing of Jane Austen, and that there were no letters preserved either of Shakespeare's or of Jane Austen's that they had

not been ripped open like pigs.'
[Mrs Cameron, Letter in *Autobiography of Henry Taylor*, 1885]

We shall adopt our own viewpoint. The letters, notwithstanding Tennyson's claim, have in a small part survived. Make of them what we will, they offer the closest opportunity of 'hearing' Jane Austen's personal 'voice'. It is perhaps fortunate that the only ones that survive are those that deal mostly with everyday rather than special events, for it is in the confident, unguarded intimacies between equals that the essence of personality may be discerned.

Some 150 letters have survived and we are fortunate that they have been scrupulously edited and documented by R.W. Chapman. Of these the first belong to the years when Jane Austen, after having already written much as a child, had produced work which her father saw fit to offer to a publisher. Most of the letters are to her sister Cassandra, who, as is so often the case in a writer's family, carefully destroyed all the controversial or unflattering items within the collection. It was natural for Jane Austen's family to be defensive, and although we may be exasperated by the loss of invaluable information, we must respect Cassandra's right to make her own decision. As Charlotte Brontë would shield her sister Emily by the same suppression of evidence so Cassandra acted in her sister's best interests, and we must remain content with what we have and be grateful for having it.

Jane Austen herself will, if we allow her, guide our response. Writing to Cassandra in 1805 with a very free pen about the final illness of a Mrs Lloyd, an old family friend, she begins with typical gossip:

> We did not walk in the Crescent (at Bath) yesterday, it was hot and crowded enough; so we went into the field, and passed close to Stephen Terry and Miss Seymour again. I have not yet seen her face but neither her dress nor air have anything of the Dash or Stillness that the Browns talked of; quite the contrary indeed, her dress is not even smart . . .
> [Letter to Cassandra, 8 April 1805]

But the letter continues:

> I received your letter last night, & wish it may soon be followed by another to say that all is over; but I cannot help thinking that Nature will struggle again & produce a revival. Poor woman! May her end be peaceful and easy . . .
> The Nonsense I have been writing in this and in my last letter, seems out of place at such a time; but I will not mind it, it will do you no harm, & nobody else will be attacked by it.

'Nobody else will be attacked by it': because the writer did not expect anyone else to read this letter. She knew that Cassandra would understand her apparent frivolity, and we must never forget that it is we who intrude, interpreting private comment as published statement.

The contrast of mood, of the frivolous with the serious, the mixing of wit and playful malice with serious comment, has led to many misreadings of the letters. If we accept Jane Austen's own caution and remember to whom she is directing her remarks, we may travel less uncomfortably through her apparent malice. Even the celebrated paragraph that delights those who seek to establish her inhumanity may appear in a different light, if we bear in mind that sister is writing to sister:

> Mrs Hall of Sherborne was brought to bed yesterday of a dead child, some weeks before she expected, owing to a fright. I suppose she happened unawares to look at her husband.
> [Letter to Cassandra, 27 October 1798]

We know, because Jane Austen has told us through Mr Knightley's admonishing of Emma when she was unforgivably rude to Miss Bates at Box Hill that such crass cruelty is inexcusable. But such remarks have less

---

Afternoon dresses of the year 1800. This type of fashion would have been typical of the time Jane was in Bath. Bath Reference Library.

The busy road, Richmond Hill, 1782. Horses often proved stubborn and difficult: 'James Digweed has had a very ugly cut . . . a young horse which he had lately purchased, and which he was trying to back into its stable;– the animal kicked him down with his forefeet, and kicked a great hole in his head' (Letter from Jane Austen, 18 December 1798.)

power to hurt when they are made in the privacy of the family, than they do when they are made directly to the person concerned.

A letter from the Bull and George inn at Dartford is typical of Jane Austen's correspondence with Cassandra in the closing years of the eighteenth century:

Bull and George
Dartford:

Wednesday, October 24 [1798]

My Dear Cassandra

You have already heard from Daniel, I conclude, in what excellent time we reached and quitted Sittingbourne, and how very well my mother bore her journey thither. I am now able to send you a continuation of the same good account of her. She was very little fatigued on her arrival at this place, has been refreshed by a comfortable dinner, and now seems quite stout. It wanted five minutes of twelve when we left Sittingbourne, from whence we had a famous pair of horses, which took us to Rochester in an hour and a quarter; the postboy seemed determined to show my

mother that Kentish drivers were not always tedious, and really drove as fast as *Caz*.

Our next stage was not quite so expeditiously performed; the road was heavy and our horses very indifferent. However, we were in such good time, and my mother bore her journey so well, that expedition was of little importance to us; and as it was, we were very little more than two hours and a half coming hither, and it was scarcely past four when we stopped at the inn. My mother took some of her bitters at Ospring, and some more at

Jane Austen often travelled by mail coach, recording in her letters to her sister the inconvenience and discomfort of this method of transport. The rutted road gives some idea of the conditions that prevailed.

Rochester, and she ate some bread several times.

We have got apartments up two pair of stairs, as we could not be otherwise accommodated with a sitting room and bed-chambers on the same floor, which we wished to be. We have one double-bedded and one single-bedded room; In the former my mother and I are to sleep. I shall leave you to guess who it is to occupy the other. We sat down to dinner a little after five, and had some beefsteaks and a boiled fowl, but no oyster sauce.

I should have begun my letter soon after our arrival but for a little adventure that prevented me. After we had been here a quarter of an hour it was discovered that my writing and dressing boxes had been by accident put into a chaise which was just packed off as we came in, and were driven away towards Gravesend on their way to the West Indies. No part of my property could have been such a prize before, for in my writing box was all my worldly wealth, £7 and my dear Harry's deputation. Mr. Nottley immediately despatched a man and horse after the chaise, and in half an hour's time I had the pleasure of being as rich as ever; they were got about two or three miles off.

My day's journey had been pleasanter in every respect than I had expected. I have been very little crowded and by no means unhappy. Your watchfulness with regard to the weather was very kind and very effectual. We had one heavy shower on leaving Sittingbourne, but afterwards the clouds cleared away, and we had a very bright *chrystal* afternoon.

My father is now reading *The Midnight Bell*, which he has got from the library, and mother is sitting by the fire. Our route tomorrow is not determined. We have none of us much inclination for London, and if Mr. Nottley will give us leave I think we shall go to Staines through Croydon and Kingston, which will be much pleasanter than the other way; but he is decidedly for Clapham and Battersea.
God bless you all!
                    Yours affectionately,
                                        J.A.
I flatter myself that *itty Dordy* will not forget me at least under a week. Kiss him for me.

In this one letter we are shown a microcosm of the Georgian way of travel, its hazards and pleasures; we hear of mother's illnesses, a constant topic in the Austen household; father's reading; and in the postscript, of the next generation of Austens. *Itty Dordy* is Edward's third child *little George* and Jane's second nephew of whom we shall hear more later.

Jane Austen's brother assured us that his sister was as good a conversationalist as she was a writer. We do not have her conversations but by good fortune in these letters we have the fossilized remains of the live events. Inadvertently the novelist makes a good social historian and in her full account of her journey we can catch her own particular voice. It is from these chronicles of family doings that we can glimpse the shadow of Jane Austen, sister, daughter and aunt, as well as aspiring writer. We must leave the last word with Jane Austen. In *Persuasion* Anne Elliot is quite eloquent on the subject of reading other people's letters:
'She was obliged to recollect that her seeing the letter was a violation of the laws of honour, that no one ought to be judged or known by such testimonies, that no private correspondence could bear the eye of others.'

The Early Writing:
1787-1793

IF YOU were a member of the Austen household at Steventon when Jane Austen was a mere twelve years old, you ran the risk of having a spoof novel or poem dedicated to you. The young Jane, between her twelfth and seventeenth birthdays, was a busy writer, and one of her particular delights was to seize upon some event in the family's life, or some handy individual who had given her an opportunity for satire, and then to mark the occasion or 'flatter' the person with a piece of writing. Of all this kind of writing twenty-nine pieces were collected by Jane Austen and preserved first by her, and after her death by her family, so that we have, in three volumes, the 'collected writings' of the years 1787 to 1793. With these pieces we also have the 'solemn' dedications: *Fragment* is dedicated to the *three month old* daughter of her eldest brother:

To Miss Jane Anna Elizabeth Austen
My Dear Niece,
Though you are at this period not many degrees removed from infancy, Yet trusting that you will in time be older, and that through the care of your excellent Parents, you will one day or another be able to read written hand, I dedicate to you the following Miscellaneous Morsels, convinced that if you seriously attend to them, You will derive from them very Important Instructions, with regard to your Conduct in Life. – If such my hopes should hereafter be realised, never shall I regret the Days and Nights that have been spent in composing these Treatises for your Benefit. I am my dear Niece
Your very affectionate
Aunt.
THE AUTHOR

No one escaped. Father, Mother, brothers and sister, even visitors as well as friends found themselves the patrons, willy-nilly, of prose, verse and, in some cases, of dramas. Writing was clearly part of a social event, an exchange between persons who had much in common.

It is improbable that the twenty-nine pieces that Jane Austen anthologized represent the whole of her writing during the five years. The range of pieces attempted and the confidence which they display indicate that they are but part of a much larger body of writing.

The Rectory at Steventon was the right place for a young writer to grow up. Plenty happened and plenty was discussed, books were to be had for reading and company for argument and the sharing of ideas. If we add to that the encouragement offered by a sympathetic and scholarly father we can form a just picture of the circumstances in which Jane's talents were fostered. The three notebooks, entitled *Volume the First*, *Volume the Second*, and *Volume the Third*, may well have been a gift to the young writer from her father. The second volume bears her signature, the date May 6th 1792, and the Latin expression, *Ex Dono Mei Patris* (Given me by my father), which confirms that the father who five years later was to send one of her novels to a London publisher, was already doing much to encourage her efforts.

However much help she might or might not have had, the minor works of her early years, or *Juvenalia* as the critics would have us call them, already display considerable skill and a fine confidence in the exploration of words and the way that they work on the page. The family that for years after her death wished to hide these early attempts from the public need not have worried. They more than adequately bear reading, being competent beyond what could be expected of one so young. Moreover, as many of them are humorous pieces they more than repay the reader for his pains. But her family's fears were keenly felt, and the need to defend the 'favourite Aunt' pressing:

Jack & Alice

a novel.

Is respectfully inscribed to Francis William Austen Esqr Midshipman on board his Majesty's Ship the Perseverance by his obedient humble Servant The Author

Chapter the first

Mr Johnson was once upon a time about 53; in a twelvemonth afterwards he was 54, which so much delighted him that he was determined to celebrate his next Birth day by giving a Masquerade to his Children & Freinds. Accordingly on the Day he attained his 55th year tickets were dispatched to all his Neighbours to that purpose. His acquaintance indeed in that part of the World were not very numerous as they consisted only of Lady

Pages from Volume the First *showing the 'spoof' dedication to Jane's brother Frank. Almost all her minor works bear light-hearted dedications to family and friends. Bodleian Library, Oxford.*

'It would be unfair to expose this preliminary process to the world, as it would be to display all that goes on behind the curtain of a theatre before it is drawn up.' Her nephew, in his memoir of his dead Aunt, was cautious about the value of the early writing:

'Her earliest stories are of a slight and flimsy texture, and are generally intended to be nonsensical, but the nonsense has much spirit in it. They are usually preceded by a dedication of mock solemnity to someone of her family. It would seem that the grandiloquent dedications prevalent in those days had not escaped her youthful penetration.'

We need not be so cautious. After nearly two hundred years these early compositions remain entertaining, reaching far beyond the family group who felt that their relevance was too closely related to their own fireside.

Without searching and straining to find the budding genius in the young girl's experiments it is still possible to see the value of writing such as this:

'Miss Dickins was an excellent Governess. She instructed me in the Paths of Virtue; under her tuition I daily became more amiable, & might perhaps by this time have nearly attained perfection, had not my worthy Preceptoress been torn from my arms, e'er I had attained my seventeenth year. I never shall forget her

last words. 'My dear Kitty she said Good night t'ye.' 'I never saw her afterwards,' continued Lady Williams wiping her eyes, 'She eloped with the Butler the same night.'

Or again in this, which describes a lovesick young man's device for leaving love letters for his beloved:

Dear Sally,

I have found a very convenient hollow oak to put our letters in; for you know we have long maintained a private Correspondence. It is about a mile from my House and seven from yours. You may perhaps imagine that I might have made a choice of tree which would have divided the Distance more equally—I was sensible of this at the time, but as I considered that the walk would be of benefit to you in your weak & uncertain state of Health, I preferred it to one nearer your House, & am yr faithfull,

Benjamin Bar.

In describing an elderly suitor's proposal, the young beginner shows an uncanny skill with words:

'Scarcely were they seated as usual, in the most affectionate manner in one chair, than the door suddenly opened and an aged gentleman with a sallow face

January, by Robert Dighton. One of a series that shows ladies' costumes for each month of the year. Victoria and Albert Museum, London.

and old pink coat, partly by intention and partly through weakness was at the feet of the lovely Charlotte, declaring his attachment to her and beseeching her pity in the most moving manner. Not being able to resolve to make anyone miserable, she consented to become his wife; whereupon the gentleman left the room and all was quiet.'

Three pieces in different works sharing the same sureness and competence. The young writer conveys her amusement and makes the comedy work in words. This art of burlesque abounds in the first volume of her early compositions. It does not matter that such burlesque was fashionable in her childhood and that she was 'merely imitating' a current mode in literary satire. She is successful, her imitations work and the pieces are entertaining.

It is worth reminding ourselves that the above passages, while illustrating the kind of subjects which the young girl chose for her writing, also read well aloud. Jane Austen wrote for the ear and not for the eye. We know that she had a fine reading voice and that she and her mother took it in turns to read her novels to family and visitor alike. But there is nothing unusual in this; it was the ordinary practice. Because we have abandoned a habit owing to the implications of our present way of life, we should not overlook commonplace occurrences of two hundred years ago and find them remarkable in their time. It was perfectly natural for Jane Austen to read to her family, in fact it would have been odd for her not to have done so. Equally it is not surprising that her writing *reads* well; that it has a rhetorical quality that benefits from being read aloud, for immediately the dramatic nature of the writing and the resonance of the words, which a lazy reading can miss, becomes apparent. Above all it is the sense of *timing* in the comic writing which is so important, and which Jane Austen managed so cleverly even in her youthful works.

The young Jane Austen clearly enjoyed herself. The sense of fun, of a happy observant child finding amusement in things, is present in every page of these early notebooks. What splendid company she must have been, but what a disarming thing so quick a sense of humour can be. From these juvenile writings, which are such light-hearted pieces, we can readily imagine the child who was soon to be in great demand as a storyteller. The exaggerations, the absurd posturing of pompous people, the undermiming of conceit; all add up to sparkling passages capable of delighting an audience.

Jane Austen's themes are not arbitrary. The attitudes which she pilloried in *Volume the First* belong to the world in which she was growing up. One of her prime targets was the Sentimental Novel, a form of popular fiction and the staple of circulating libraries, that was so easy to parody. Easy, that is, if you were a competent writer. The hallmark of such writing was exaggeration and extremes. Heroines fell instantly in love, heroes were dashing, wealthy and winnable, and the whole world of the fiction turned upon the whims of the author. Plots could be twisted any way in order to speed the action along and incongruity, far from being a disadvantage, was a valuable device for shocking the reader or creating a sudden resolution to a tangled tale. Resourcefulness and astonishing good fortune were the chief attributes of the heroes and heroines of these swooning and swash-buckling tales. Jane Austen's mischievous pen could catch the style to the letter:

'No sooner had Eliza entered her dungeon than the first thought which occurred to her was how to get out of it again.

She went to the door; but it was locked. She looked at the window; but it was barred with iron; disappointed in both her expectations, she despaired of effecting her Escape, when she fortunately perceived in a corner of her cell, a small saw and ladder of ropes. With the saw she instantly went to work and in a few weeks had displaced every bar but one to which she fastened the ladder.

A difficulty then occurred which for some time, she knew not how to obviate. Her children were too small to get down the ladder by themselves, nor would it be possible for her to take them in her arms, when *she* did. At last she determined to fling down all her clothes, of which she had a large quantity, and then having given them strict charge not to hurt themselves, threw her children after them. She herself with ease descended by the ladder, at the bottom of which she had the pleasure of finding her little boys in perfect health and fast asleep.

Her wardrobe she now saw a fatal necessity of selling, both for the preservation of her children and herself. With tears in her eyes, she parted with these last reliques of her former glory, and with the money she got for them, bought others more useful, some playing things for her boys and a gold watch for herself.

But scarcely was she provided with the above mentioned necessaries, than she began to find herself rather hungry, and had reason to think, by their biting off two of her fingers, that her children were much in the same situation.'

Here the farfetched adventures of a typical sentimental novel's heroine are admirably mocked. Interestingly the prose is successful, the sentences are poised and because of this the comedy works. There is a sure hand at work employing the genre and its style of writing to great effect.

Young writers need practice, above all with vocabulary. Words are what writers work with and it is the good humoured, almost 'heady' playing with language that gives him confidence. A feature of much writing by

Below: The History of England, *a satirical history by Jane in her own hand and illustrated by her sister Cassandra.* British Library, London.

Above: A Young Ladies Instructor. *The kind of book that Jane Austen parodied in her youthful exuberant satires. Mrs R. M. Lefroy.*

Malton's View near Bath, *1785. It was along just
such a road that Jane and her family made the journey
to Bath, their luggage in the basket at the back of the
coach. Jane records journeys during the course of
which the coach had to stop to have wheels greased,
additional horses had to be harnessed because roads
were so bad, and the passengers were obliged to walk
up a hill, often arriving at the top long before the
coach itself. Victoria Art Gallery, Bath.*

the young is the use made of lists, and Jane Austen is no
exception. But she takes an impish delight in twisting
the tails of the lists she uses:

'Mr Clifford lived at Bath; and having never seen
London, set off one Monday morning determined to
feast his eyes with a sight of that great Metropolis. He
travelled in his coach and four, for he was a very rich
young man and kept a great many carriages of which I
did not recollect half. I can only remember that he had a
coach, a chariot, a chaise, a landau, a landaulet, a
phaeton, a gig, a whiskey, an Italian chair, a buggy, a
curricle, and a wheelbarrow. He had likewise an
amazing fine stud of horses. To my knowledge he had six
greys, four bays, eight blacks and a pony.'

The effect of this list is comic in a way that is not rare in
Jane Austen's work: the 'wheelbarrow' provides an
exquisite absurdity to the whole catalogue of enviable
possessions. Again and again such accurate and joyful
games with words appear:

'Sir William Mountague was the son of Sir Henry
Mountague, who was the son of Sir John Mountague, a
descendant of Sir Christopher Mountague, who was the
nephew of Sir Edward Mountague, whose ancestor was
Sir James Mountague a near relation of Sir Robert
Mountague, who inherited the Title and estate of Sir
Fredrick Mountague.'

This kind of joke is still popular with script writers for
screen, radio and television.

Perhaps the most splendid example, which also
illustrates Jane Austen's developing sense of the silliness
of fashions, comes in *The Three Sisters*, a novel set out in
the form of letters, one of the longer pieces in *Volume the
First*. A young lady and her mother explain to a would-
be husband his obligations:

44

"'And remember I am to have a new carriage hung as high as the Dutton's, & blue spotted with silver; and I shall expect a new saddle horse, a suit of fine lace, and an infinite number of the most valuable jewels. Diamonds such as never were seen, (Pearls as large as those of the Princess Badroulbadour in the 4th volume of the Arabian Nights and rubies, emeralds, topazes, sapphires, amethysts, turkeystones, agate, beads, bugles and garnets) and pearls, rubies, emeralds and beads out of number. You must set up your phaeton which must be cream coloured with a wreath of silver flowers round it, You must buy four of the finest bays in the kingdom and you must drive me in it every day. This is not all; you must entirely new furnish your house after my taste, you must hire two more footmen to attend me, two women to wait on me, must always let me do just as I please and make a very good husband."

Here she stopped, I believe rather out of breath.

"This is all very reasonable Mr Watts for my daughter to expect."

"And it is very reasonable Mrs Stanhope that your daughter should be disappointed."

He was going on but Mary interrupted him, "You must build me an elegant greenhouse, and stock it with plants. You must let me spend every winter in Bath, every Spring in Town, every Summer in taking some tour, and every autumn at a watering place, and if we are at home the rest of the year" (Sophy and I laughed) "you must do nothing but give balls and masquerades. You must build a room on purpose and a theatre to act plays in the first play we have shall be *Which is the Man* and I will do Lady Bellbloomer."

"And pray Miss Stanhope (said Mr Watts) what am I to expect from you in return for all this?"

"Expect? why you may expect to have me pleased."'

Here we can see much of Jane Austen's comedy. The subject is her favourite, to do with matchmaking, and the outline situation is typical of her imagination. The outlandish, preposterous demands of the lady are set against a mild economic enquiry on the part of the man. The writer's own standpoint is eloquent; the reader sees the comic situation for the juxtaposition is plain. But he might also have an uneasy feeling that the extreme case being presented is not too far from reality in many such situations. We all from time to time submit to the claims of fashion.

The majority of Jane Austen's jokes—and that is after all what a large number of her early pieces of writing are—work because they are simple. They merely take the meaning of words and behaviour and move that meaning along a little, thereby pointing to a possibility or implication that is funny. A Mr Williams, who features in *The Generous Curate*, is described in the process of launching his children in the world:

'The eldest had been placed at the Royal Academy for Seaman at Portsmouth when about thirteen years old, and from thence he had been discharged on board of one of the Vessels of a small fleet destined for Newfoundland, where his promising and amiable disposition had procured him many friends among the Natives, & from whence he regularly sent home a large Newfoundland Dog every month to his family.'

The Prince Regent cutting a dashing figure as he drives a curricle, the 'sports car' of the eighteenth century.

The Betweenities
and the History of England

Dᴜʀɪɴɢ the family debate over the publication of Jane Austen's 'slight and flimsy' early writings, Anna Lefroy, perhaps the favourite niece, who herself aspired to write, felt that the early novels should not be made available to the public. These she called the *Betweenities*, referring to the more extended pieces of writing in Jane's three notebooks, and the fragments of novels which remained unfinished at her Aunt's death.

Of these works two repay reading for their own intrinsic merit, displaying in different ways aspects of the author's imaginative powers and literary grasp. The one is *Love and Friendship*, the other, the well-known *History of England*. *Love and Friendship* is an irreverent mockery of the sentimental novel in letters, while *The History of England* is a comic parody of the historical anthology popular in eighteenth-century England.

Dedicated to her cousin La Comtesse De Feuillide, *Love and Friendship* is sub-titled:

'Deceived in Friendship & Betrayed in Love'
and it abounds with swooning heroines coping with that central concern of women in such novels: the moment when the possibility of marriage crosses their path. In this work Jane Austen allowed her mischievous sense of fun free rein and caught precisely the style of the stories which she was mocking:

'As the daughter of my most intimate friend I think you entitled to that knowledge of my unhappy story, which your mother has so often solicited me to give you.

My father was a native of Ireland and an inhabitant of Wales; my mother was the natural daughter of a Scotch peer by an Italian Opera girl–I was born in Spain and received my education at a convent in France.'
The sentimental novel was notorious for such extravaganza; its plots were far-fetched, its characters far removed from any semblance of reality. It is worth noting that Jane Austen's mature works were to be the very opposite of the novels which she so deftly parodies. But the imitation and the jokes proved a fertile ground for the apprentice writer. A further letter from *Love and Friendship* shows Jane Austen playing yet another game with words:

'One evening in December, as my Father, my Mother and myself, were arranged in social converse round our fireside, we were on a sudden, greatly astonished, by hearing a violent knocking on the outward Door of our rustic Cot.

My Father started–"What noise is that," (said he.) "It sounds like a loud rapping at the door"–(replied my Mother.) "It does indeed." (cried I.) "I am of your opinion; (said my Father) it certainly does appear to proceed from some uncommon violence exerted against our unoffending door." "Yes (exclaimed I) I cannot help thinking it must be somebody who knocks for admittance."

"That is another point (replied he;) We must not pretend to determine on what motive the person may knock–though that someone *does* rap at the door, I am partly convinced."

Here, a second tremendous rap interrupted my Father in his speech and somewhat alarmed my Mother and me.

"Had we not better go and see who it is? (said she) the servants are out." "I think we had." (replied I.) "Certainly, (added my Father) by all means." "Shall we go now?" (said my Mother,) "The sooner the better" (answered he). "Oh let no time be lost" (cried I).

A third more violent Rap than ever again assaulted our ears. "I am certain there is somebody knocking at the door." (said my Mother.) "I think there must," (replied my Father.) "I fancy the servants are returned; (said I) I think I hear Mary going to the door." "I am glad of it (cried my Father) for I long to know who it is."'

A plate from the magazine Ackerman's Repository
showing ladies' evening opera dresses of the year 1810.
Bath Reference Library.

There can be no doubt of the success of such writing; as a script for the Steventon theatricals it would serve well. As it is, it works.

In *A Collection of Letters* found in *Volume the Second*, the dedication to Jane Cooper, her friend from her Reading schooldays, announces the kind of writing we are to expect:

Cousin
Conscious of the Charming Character which in every Country, and every Clime in Christendom is Cried, Concerning you, with Caution and Care I Commend to your Charitable Criticism this Clever Collection of Curious Comments, which have been Carefully Culled, Collected and Classed by your Comical Cousin

The Author.

In the story, Maria Williams, who sends the letters, tells of her 'adventures' at the hands of various people. She is an early version of Jane Austen's later heroines, and some of the people that she has to deal with are skilfully drawn characters:

'I soon forgot all my vexations in the pleasure of dancing and of having the most agreeable partner in the whole room. As he is moreover heir to a very large estate I could see that Lady Greville did not look very well pleased when she found who had been his choice. – She was determined to mortify me, and accordingly when we were sitting down between the dances, she came to me with *more* than her usual insulting importance attended by Miss Mason and said loud enough to be heard by half the people in the room, 'Pray Miss Maria in what way of business was your Grandfather? for Miss Mason and I cannot agree whether he was a

Fashion of the year 1786, the time when Jane was beginning to write her earliest satires. Such may have been the clothes worn by her early heroes and heroines. Victoria and Albert Museum, London.

This work, 'By a partial, prejudiced, & ignorant Historian' is probably the most well known of all the juvenile writings. Dedicated to her sister Cassandra, who is assured that, 'there will be very few Dates in this History', it is a light-hearted outline of thirteen monarchs. In *Volume the Second* there is a set of water colour illustrations done by Cassandra Austen, which complement the text. Two examples will serve to show the kind of 'history' it was that the sisters produced. The first extract is about Henry IV:

'Henry the 4th ascended the throne of England much to his own satisfaction in the year 1399, after having prevailed on his cousin & predecessor Richard the 2nd, to resign it to him, & to retire for the rest of his life to Pomfret Castle where he happened to be murdered. It is to be supposed that Henry was married, since he had certainly four sons, but it is not in my power to inform the Reader who was his wife. Be this as it may, he did not live for ever, but falling ill, his son the Prince of Wales came and took away the crown; whereupon the King made a long speech, for which I must refer the Reader to Shakespeare's Plays, and the Prince made a still longer.

A book illustration that shows the departure, perhaps on a moonlit night, for the ballroom. A common scene in Jane Austen's life as well as in her fiction.

Grocer or a Bookbinder.' I saw that she wanted to mortify me and was resolved if I possibly could to prevent her seeing that her scheme succeeded. . . . 'I believe not Ma'am.' 'Did not he abscond?' 'I never heard that he did.' 'At least he died insolvent?' 'I was never told so before.' 'Why was not your father as poor as a rat?' 'I fancy not.' 'Was not he in the King's Bench once?' 'I never saw him there.' She gave me *such* a look, and turned away in a great passion; while I was half delighted with myself for my impertinence, and half afraid of being thought too saucy. As Lady Greville was extremely angry with me, she took no further notice of me all evening.'

Lady Greville's malice and Maria's spirited replies during the *attack* in the ballroom were later to become the substance of Jane Austen's invention. Here they are already deployed most skilfully. The social setting, the snobbery, the whole tone and manner of the proceedings gives us a foretaste of the fuller inventions that were to follow.

Unfinished sketch of Jane Austen by her sister Cassandra. This is the only authentic likeness of the author. National Portrait Gallery, London.

A lady prepares her head-dress for a ball. The moon in the window shows that it would be possible to travel that night. Fashions went to extremes during Jane's lifetime and were much satirized in cartoons and in fiction.

Things being thus settled between them the King died and was succeeded by his son Henry who had previously beat Sir William Gascoigne.'

The second is about Queen Mary:

'This woman had the good luck of being advanced to the throne of England, in spite of the superior pretensions, Merit, and Beauty of her Cousins Mary Queen of Scotland and Jane Grey. Nor can I pity the Kingdom for the misfortunes they experienced during her Reign, since they fully deserved them, for having allowed her to succeed her brother – which was a double piece of folly, since they might have foreseen that as she died without children, she would be succeeded by that disgrace to humanity, that pest to society, Elizabeth. Many were the people who fell martyrs to the protestant Religion during her reign; I suppose not fewer than a dozen. She married Philip King of Spain who in her sister's reign was famous for building Armadas. She died without issue, and then the dreadful moment came in which the destroyer of all comfort, the deceitful Betrayer of trust reposed in her, and the Murderess of her Cousin succeeded to the Throne.'

Thus the sixteen-year-old girl comically chronicled the 'History of England'.

VOLUME THE THIRD

As we might expect the third volume of the notebooks is made up of more substantial pieces of writing: the 'novel' *Evelyn* still in letter form and the longest piece of all, *Catherine*, which was dedicated to Cassandra:

To Miss Austen
Madam
Encouraged by your warm patronage of The Beautiful Cassandra, and the History of Eng-

land, which through your generous support, have obtained a place in every Library in the Kingdom, and run through threescore Editions, I take the liberty of begging the same Exertions in favour of the following Novel, which I humbly flatter myself, possesses Merit beyond any already published, or any that will in future appear, except such as may proceed from the pen of Your Most Grateful Humble Servt

THE AUTHOR

Steventon August 1792

Catherine, perhaps more than any other of these early works, bears many hints of the way that Jane Austen's talent was to develop. Here, already, can be seen the themes, situations and subtleties of character that so enrich her later writing. The 'girlish' fun and delight in the preoccupation of 'young ladies' with flirtation, courtship and the possibilities of marriage, establishes the pattern of prose that Jane Austen was to make supremely her own as she matured. The opening of this early 'novel' has all the poise and confidence of mature writing:

'Catherine had the misfortune as many heroines had before her, of losing her Parents when she was very young, and of being brought up under the care of a Maiden Aunt, who while she tenderly loved her, watched over her conduct with so scrutinizing a severity, as to make it very doubtful to many people, and to Catherine amongst the rest, whether she loved her or not. She had frequently been deprived of a real pleasure through this jealous Caution, had been sometimes obliged to relinquish a Ball because an Officer was to be there, or to dance with a Partner of her Aunt's introduction in preference to one of her own Choice.'

Here we have the ingredients of Jane Austen's art. The heroine must do battle with her own will and understanding of things and the pressures of society which are felt through the exertions of those close to her. The challenge of courtship in that genteel battlefield of love's war, the ballroom, and the significance of 'one's own choice' herald the great campaigns of later Assemblies and the agonized deliberations between propriety and desire that Jane Austen's heroines endure.

One of the most startling features of Jane Austen's writing is the clarity with which she faces up to the realities of life. Because her works are primarily concerned with the exercise of reason, and are 'reflective' rather than packed with violent action, it is easy to imagine that she has little sense of the so-called 'real' nature of life. It is as if her 'elegance' somehow removes all possibility of her ever being a 'flesh and blood' human being herself. Careful reading however, as in most cases, suggests that such a judgement is not only

hasty but quite erroneous. Although physical violence is kept firmly away from her novels, physicality, in the sense that people are shown as vulnerable creatures, permeates her writing. Her heroines can catch cold, and in this story, Catherine succumbs to toothache. Promised a Ball, she retires to bed in high spirits:
'. . . but Kitty awoke the next Morning with a violent Toothake [*sic*]. It was in vain that she endeavoured at first to deceive herself; her feelings were witnesses too acute of its reality; with as little success did she try to sleep it off, for the pain she suffered prevented her closing her Eyes–. She then summoned her Maid and with the Assistance of the Housekeeper, every remedy that the receipt book or the head of the latter contained, was tried, but ineffectually; for though for a short time relieved by them, the pain still returned. She was now obliged to give up the endeavour, and to reconcile herself not only to the pain of Toothake, but to the loss of a Ball; . . .'

Almost unwittingly Jane Austen is an excellent social historian, showing us in this piece of fiction an easily overlooked disadvantage of life in Georgian England two hundred years ago.

But it is in her companion's response to Kitty's disappointment that the true Jane Austen is to be seen. Camilla, who has also been invited to the Ball, comments upon Kitty's misfortune in such a way that Jane Austen leaves us in no doubt about the young lady's chief concern:
'"To be sure, there never was anything so shocking, said Camilla; to come on such a day too! For one would not have minded it you know had it been at *any other* time. But it is always so. I never was at a Ball in my Life, but what something happened to prevent somebody from going! I wish there were no such things as Teeth in the World; they are nothing but plagues to one, and I dare say that People might easily invent something to eat with instead of them; Poor Thing! What pain you are in! I declare it is quite Shocking to look at you. But you won't have it out, will you? For Heaven's sake don't; for there is nothing I dread so much. I declare I had rather undergo the greatest Tortures in the World than have a tooth drawn. Well! how patiently you bear it! how can you be so quiet? Lord, if I were in your place I should make such a fuss, there would be no bearing me. I should torment you to Death."
"So you do, as it is," thought Kitty.'

The mock sympathy, the concern with health, the exquisite self-centredness of Camilla, Kitty's quiet thought at the end of the 'conversation', all are features which show the qualities we applaud and are moved by in *Emma* and *Persuasion*. Jane Austen's vision is so clear, her irony so deftly portrayed, that in so early a 'novel' we can but admire the economy of words with which she describes Camilla as she prepares to depart for the Ball leaving Kitty at home:
'Mrs Stanley & her daughter appeared, and Camilla in high Spirits, & perfect good humour with her own looks, was more violent than ever in her lamentations over her Friend as she practised her Scotch Steps about the room.'
The irony has the edge of a scalpel. At seventeen Jane Austen was making words work for her with a precision that was to become more acute with her maturity.

The 'old copy book containing several tales, some of which seems to have been composed while she was quite a girl', which her nephews and nieces were hesitant over publishing after her death, is a treasure chest. Its twenty-nine pieces gathered from who can tell however many more tell us clearly, across the years, that for the young girl writing was enormous fun. She wrote to delight her family and friends, and quite clearly, out of her own delight. Little seems to have escaped the eyes and ears of the twelve-year-old Jane. We can well believe the nephews and nieces who tell us of the peals of laughter that they heard from behind the door where Aunt Jane and Aunt Cassandra Austen were telling each other stories.

*Above: The Tapestry Room at Osterley Park,
believed by many to be one of Robert Adam's finest
designs. Adam designs, perhaps more than any others,
display the elegance and style achieved by the wealthy
in England in the late eighteenth century.*

*Opposite top: The iron bridge over the River Severn
near Coalbrookdale. The bridge, finished in 1779
when Jane Austen was four years old, was the first
large bridge to be built entirely of cast iron.
Throughout her life the manufacturing processes that
this bridge symbolizes gradually transformed man's
relationship with nature. Jane Austen's death at forty-
two meant that she never saw the full implications of
the great industrial and commercial revolution that
would eventually challenge all her assumptions about
civilization.*

*Opposite bottom: A view over Bath, 1789, by Parker.
It was over just such a view of Bath that the Tilney
brother and sister in* Northanger Abbey *occupied
themselves 'viewing the country with the eyes of
persons accustomed to drawing and decided on its
capability of being formed into pictures, with all the
eagerness of real taste'. An activity that Jane Austen
gently satirizes through the commonsense view of
Catherine, who found the 'picturesque' interpretation of
the landscape a complete contradiction to what she saw
with her own eyes. Victoria Art Gallery, Bath.*

Hampshire Society

WE CAN never know what life in Steventon Rectory was like in Hampshire in the eighteenth century. As generations of historians piece together the patchwork of surviving information the details of their discoveries constantly remind us of how little we can know with confidence.

Our knowledge of Jane Austen's novels, the very freshness or 'modern' quality of her writing can, while delighting us, delude us into feeling that we know her and her circumstances well. Eighteenth century Hampshire is now a long way away from us in time, and the style and preoccupations of life in Steventon more remote than we believe.

Throughout the eighteenth century Hampshire was a county where many of the changes and concerns of the whole nation could be seen. During the period of the wars with France, Hampshire was particularly sensitive about invasion, being vulnerable through Portsmouth and having direct routes to London. During recession in the wool trade a town like Alton would be hard hit and during times of bad harvests the large rural areas would become areas of considerable hardship. The landscape and the nature of the terrain would dictate the circumstances in which people found themselves. Proximity to Portsmouth would bring deforestation as the oak trees went for the making of ships, as well as trade deriving from provisions for the fleet. But proximity to Portsmouth would also bring the press gang, and smuggling with all its attendant disturbances.

The concern with literature, scholarship, family affairs and fashion that we find in Jane Austen's letters from Steventon must be set against the larger landscape of the county in which she lived. When Jane Austen tells us that she *once* walked alone from Steventon to Deane, some two-and-a-half miles, we should pause to reflect upon the reasons why she did not walk alone more often. It was no feeble whim that led Jane Austen to walk accompanied, nor the observance of etiquette. It simply was not safe to go about on one's own. There is a splendid example in *Emma* of the very real difficulty that young ladies could find themselves in:

'Miss Smith, and Miss Bickerton . . . had walked out together, and taken a road – the Richmond road, which though apparently public enough for safety, had led them into alarm. About half a mile beyond Highbury, making a sudden turn, and deeply shaded by elms on each side, it became for a considerable stretch very retired; and when the young ladies had advanced some way into it, they had suddenly perceived at a small distance before them, . . . a party of gipsies. A child on the watch came towards them to beg; and Miss Bickerton, excessively frightened, gave a great scream, and calling on Harriet to follow her, ran up a steep bank, cleared a slight hedge at the top, and made the best of her way by a short cut back to Highbury. But poor Harriet could not follow. She had suffered very much from cramp after dancing, and her first attempt to mount the bank brought on such a return of it as made her absolutely powerless – and in this state, and exceedingly terrified, she had been obliged to remain.

How the trampers might have behaved, had the young ladies been more courageous, must be doubtful; but such an invitation for attack could not be resisted; and Harriet was soon assailed by half a dozen children, headed by a stout woman and a great boy, all clamorous and impertinent in look, though not absolutely in word. More and more frightened, she immediately promised them money, and taking out her purse, gave them a shilling, and begged them not to want more, or to use her ill. She was then able to walk, though but slowly, and was moving away – but her terror and her purse were too tempting, and she was followed, or rather surrounded, by the whole gang, demanding more.' [Vol. III Chapter III]

Harriet had not been bred to rule; this was a novel however, and her plight was not too desperate. Help, in the shape of Frank Churchill, was around the corner. In real life in eighteenth-century Hampshire, gipsies and vagabonds presented a real danger. The episode in the story underlines Jane Austen's comments about her unusual solitary walk. Civilization belonged to 'safe' roads and communities, beyond which it was not wise to venture. The picture of life in the remote country village of Steventon must include the shadowy figures of organized bands of poachers as well as groups of vagrants. Jane Austen, with typical restraint, reminds us in *Emma* of what might lie beyond the turn in the road. Interestingly it is the raid on the poultry houses in Emma's neighbourhood and the stealing of all the turkeys that persuades her father, on the last page of the novel, to consent to his daughter's marriage. From history we know that the thieves if caught would have been hanged for the birds that they took.

If man's presence in a wooded rural landscape was a deterrent to young ladies walking out, a further more limiting hindrance was the weather. Jane Austen, writing to her sister, comments:

> There has been a great deal of rain here for this last fortnight, much more than in Kent, and indeed we found the roads all the ways from Staines most disgracefully dirty. Steven-

ton lane has its full share of it, and I don't know when I shall be able to get to Deane.
[Letter to Cassandra, 27 October 1798]

Such a comment is commonplace in her correspondence. It was the custom to wear pattens, a form of slip-on wooden or metal platform to lift ordinary footwear above the mud, when the lanes were 'very sloppy' as Jane Austen aptly described them. It is from details such as these that we can build a partial picture of life in and around her home. Walking was one means of travel, another was the horse-drawn carriage. We can find references to the Austen family travelling but we also have other accounts of conditions in Hampshire to draw upon.

Not far from Steventon was the village of Selborne where from 1720 until 1793 Gilbert White lived and recorded his observations of 'nature' which were to be published as *The Natural History of Selborne*. In this collection of letters we can find much that is relevant for a study of Jane Austen's formative years, while glimpsing some of the splendid eccentricities that early science encouraged. The account White gives us of an experiment he performed to ascertain whether bees possess the

---

Portsmouth, home of the navy to which Jane's brothers belonged. Winchester Public Library.

Above: Sporting print by Rowlandson, 1798. Horse power provides the most significant image of Jane Austen's times. She lived and wrote in a world dominated by the horse as the sole means of overland transport, a means as unreliable as it was picturesque: 'Eliza caught her cold on Sunday in our way to the D'Entraigues; – the Horses actually gibbed on this side of Hyde Park Gate – a load of fresh gravel made it a formidable Hill to them, and they refused the collar; – I believe there was a sore shoulder to irritate. – Eliza was frightened, & we got out – & were detained in the Evening air several minutes.' (Letter to Cassandra, 25 April 1811.)

Opposite top: The parlour at Chawton Cottage, which some say is the room where Jane did her writing. Over by the fireplace on the left-hand side is what is believed to be her writing table. The dinner service in the foreground is the Wedgwood set the purchase of which she mentions in a letter.

Opposite bottom: Portrait painted on plaster by John Meirs around 1809 of Jane Austen's only sister Cassandra.

An illustration from Gilbert White's Natural
History of Selborne, *showing the nature of the
Hampshire countryside in which Jane grew up.*

faculty of hearing will serve to indicate our remoteness from the eighteenth century:

'It does not appear from experiment that bees are in any way capable of being affected by sounds: for I have often tried my own with a large speaking-trumpet held close to their hives, and with such an exertion of voice as would have hailed a ship at the distance of a mile, and still these insects pursued their various employments undisturbed, and without showing the least sensibility or resentment.'

But White tells of more than good-tempered bees. His 'History' tells of marauding bands of poachers, of a leper who lived in his village (a village not far from Steventon), and of the conditions of the poor as well as the poultry of the village. It is White who tells us graphically of the baby Jane Austen's very first January. 1776 saw one of the great frosts of the eighteenth century. The month-old Jane would have to be cosseted against conditions that White found worth recording:

'Snow driving all the day, which was followed by frost, sleet and some snow, till the twelfth, when a prodigious mass overwhelmed all the works of men, drifting over the tops of the gates and filling the hollow lanes.

On the 14th the writer was obliged to be very much abroad; and he thinks he never before or since had encountered such rugged Siberian weather. Many of the narrow roads were now filled above the tops of the hedges; through which the snow was driven into most romantic and grotesque shapes, so striking to the imagination as not to be seen without wonder and pleasure. The poultry dared not stir out of their roosting-places; for cocks and hens are so dazzled and confounded by the glare of the snow that they would soon perish without assistance. The hares also lay sullenly in their seats, and would not move until compelled by hunger . . .'

But it was not only the hares who were unable to stir: 'From the 14th the snow continued to increase, and began to stop the road waggons and coaches, which could no longer keep on their regular stages, and especially on the western roads, where the fall appears to have been deeper than in the south. The company at Bath, that wanted to attend the Queen's birthday, were strangely incommoded; many carriages of persons, who got, in their way to town from Bath, as far as Marlborough, after strange embarrassments, here met with a *ne plus ultra*. The ladies fretted, and offered large rewards to labourers, if they would shovel them a track to London; but the relentless heaps of snow were too bulky to be removed; . . .'

One wonders how the family at Steventon fared with their new baby and with their own farm animals to be 'assisted'.

White concludes with a striking description of London under snow:

'. . . a sort of Laplandian-scene, very wild and grotesque indeed. But the metropolis itself exhibited a still more singular appearance. than the country; for, being bedded deep in snow, the pavement of the streets could not be touched by the wheels or the horses' feet, so that the carriages ran about without the least noise.

Such an exception from din and clatter was strange, but not pleasant; it seemed to convey an uncomfortable idea of desolation . . .'

White's description finds an echo in *Emma* where the valetudinarian Mr Woodhouse is panicked by a fall of snow. He is being teased by a bad tempered John Knightley:

'"I admired your resolution very much, sir," said he, "in venturing out in such weather, for of course you saw there would be snow very soon. Everybody must have seen the snow coming on. I admired your spirit; and I dare say we shall get home very well. Another hour or two's snow can hardly make the road impassable; and we are two carriages; if *one* is blown over in the bleak part of the common field there will be the other at hand . . .

. . . The carriages came: and Mr. Woodhouse, always the first object on such occasions, was carefully attended to his own by Mr. Knightley and Mr. Weston; but not all that either could say could prevent some renewal of alarm at the sight of the snow which had actually fallen, and the discovery of a much darker night than he had been prepared for. "He was afraid they should have a very bad drive . . . They must keep as much together as they could;" and James was talked to, and given a charge to go very slow and wait for the other carriage.' [Vol. I, Chapter XV]

The gentle teasing of the old man is comic, John Knightley has caused alarm where there was no need, moreover the snow, like the gipsies who threaten Harriet, is a fiction. The story-tale world is benevolent. In reality travelling about Hampshire could be difficult if not dangerous. The 'hollow lanes' that White describes, which were so worn down by carts and carriages that they lay some sixteen feet below the surface of the bordering fields, would be rutted and bumpy offering no easy passage for wheeled transport.

White's Hampshire with its leper, its bands of night-hunters waging battle with the keepers of the deer parks, with its poor who made themselves rush lights from 'the scummings of their bacon pot', is the background

Box Hill, the setting for the picnic in Emma, *the famous occasion on which Mr Knightley admonishes Emma for her unkindness.*

Left: Full Dress, *an illustration from* Miroir de la Mode, *1803. Like any young lady Jane Austen followed changes in fashion. Her letters give very detailed accounts of dresses which she wore, had made, would have liked to wear and saw others wearing. Details such as these provide a wealth of information for the social historian on manners as well as costume.*
Bath Reference Library.

Right: Seaside Bathing Dress, *1815. Jane Austen satirized the fast growing habit of sea-bathing, although she herself bathed in the sea: 'The sea air and sea bathing together were nearly infallible, one or the other of them being a match for every disorder, of the stomach, the lungs or the blood; they were anti-spasmodic, anti-pulmonary, anti-septic, anti-bilious & anti-rheumatic . . . They were healing, softening, relaxing, – fortifying and bracing – seemingly just as wanted – sometimes one, sometimes the other.'*
(Sanditon, *Chapter 2.*) *Bath Reference Library.*

THE FIVE POSITIONS OF DANCING.

The Figures shew the positions of the Learner,
and the Feet that of a finish'd Dancer.

Frontispiece of Wilson's Analysis of Country
Dancing, *1811, showing the five positions of dancing.
As well as indicating the dance-step, the illustration
shows the fashions of the day.*

61

against which Jane Austen lived. For her as for White communication was difficult, depending as it did upon the unreliable ways of men and the hazards of nature. Setting out to pay a social call would have been quite an undertaking. Mr Woodhouse's anxiety was not altogether without cause.

Jane Austen is explicit in her writing about the hazards confronting the traveller, and in her letters she often gives us useful details of the difficulties. It is in the opening of an unfinished work which we now know as *Sanditon*, that she brings her experience and assumptions closest to White's description of Hampshire:
'A gentleman and lady travelling from Tonbridge towards that part of the Sussex coast that lies between Hastings and Eastbourne, being induced by business to quit the high road, and attempt a very rough lane, were overturned in toiling up its long ascent half rock, half sand. The accident happened just beyond the only gentleman's house near the lane–a house, which, their driver on first being required to take that direction, had conceived to be necessarily their object, and had with most unwilling looks been constrained to pass by. He had grumbled and shaken his shoulders so much indeed, and pitied and cut his horses so sharply, that he might have been open to the suspicion of overturning them on purpose (especially as the carriage was not his master's own) if the road had not indisputably become considerably worse than before . . . as soon as the premises of the said house were left behind–expressing with a most intelligent portentous countenance that beyond it no wheels but cartwheels could safely proceed. The severity of the fall was broken by their slow pace and the narrowness of the lane . . .' [Chapter I]

We shall see that Jane Austen in her maturity knew such occurrences as commonplace, they are not merely inventions for her writing. When she and her parents left Steventon to live in Bath it was decided that they might as well sell the Steventon furniture and have more made at Bath, as it was doubtful whether the furniture would survive the journey.

VISITING

Jane and Cassandra Austen had many friends in Hampshire. There was no shortage of girls with whom they could compose and compare fashions and hairstyles, nor was there any shortage of eligible young men. However 'sloppy' the lane or cloudy the moonless nights might be, visits were made and returned. Friendships were formed that lasted for many years. While the dignified social round of the country parson was maintained, the less sedate doings of young ladies were also afoot:

> Martha has promised to return with me, and
> our plan is to have a nice black frost for
> walking to Whitechurch, and there throw

Joseph Haydn. Haydn's visits to England between the years 1791 and 1795 as recorded in his chronicles and letters give us eye-witness accounts of London, Bath and Hampshire. Haydn's piano sonatas, symphonies and choral works provide the musical background to Jane Austen's world. His oratorio The Creation *was intended as a positive statement in a world ravaged by the terrors of destructive excess in post-revolutionary France. The poise of his music may be seen as similar to the poise of Jane Austen's novels: it is social, elegant and optimistic.*

ourselves into a postchaise, one upon the other, our heads hanging out at one door, and our feet at the opposite.
[Letter to Cassandra, 30 November 1800]
Whatever the preoccupations of the Rev George Austen and his fellow clergy in the parsonages which he visited it is apparent that the daughters of those households were quite happily occupied with their own affairs.

From the monarch at court to the successful farmer in his drawing room, social visiting in England in the eighteenth century meant music in some form or other. In the court of George III Haydn would present his latest symphonies and sonatas, in the farmer's drawing room, the favoured daughter would accompany her 'improved' voice upon the piano. From time to time in court and drawing room there would be dancing. The ballroom, the musical evening, the card-playing parties, were, all over England, the pastimes of the leisured classes: no less in Hampshire than anywhere else.

Visiting, the belonging to a social 'circle', has been seen by some social historians as one of the subtle but nevertheless important strengths of English society. The mixing of people of different ranks, for whatever reason

Above: A scene in a card room where a game of whist is being played. Cards were popular with the older generation in Jane's novels.

Below: A caricature of the waltz, a dance that was causing a scandal. Most dances were of the country dance kind with sets of people. The waltz was different: 'I felt that if I were married my wife should waltz (or 'roll') with no-one but myself. Judge–The Male places the palms of his hands gently against the sides of the Female not far from the arm pits. The Female does the same. And instantly with as much velocity as possible they turn round and at the same time gradually glide round the room'. (Crabbe Robinson in Germany in 1800.) Victoria and Albert Museum, London.

Cassandra's illustrations to her sister's parody
History of England, *to be found in* Volume the
Second, *one of three surviving volumes of Jane
Austen's early writings. Here are shown* Elizabeth
(not one of Jane's favourite queens); Edward IV;
and Henry V. *Of the latter Jane wrote: 'This
Prince after he succeeded to the throne grew quite
reformed and amiable, forsaking all his dissipated
companions, and never thrashing Sir William again.
During his reign, Lord Cobham was burnt alive, but I
forget what for.' British Library, London.*

The cartoonist's view of ladies in a hat shop. Jane and her sister Cassandra spent much time shopping and keeping in touch with changes in fashion, and Jane's letters record many shopping excursions.

that it takes place, can ameliorate the suffering that inequality brings. People meeting can provoke discussion and the exchange of attitudes and ideas. It was precisely this aspect of English society that impressed Haydn when he visited London. In Vienna, Haydn was a court servant; whereas in England he found that he could not only dine with the King and Queen but could speak to them and be included in conversation. Furthermore when he presented bills to the King, for his professional services, he found that they were actually paid.

From this 'highest circle', one of glittering elegance and great wealth, a chain of such 'circles' spread across the land. As the King and Queen would entertain those of inferior rank to themselves, as well as visiting monarchs, so nobility would include gentry in their circle, and so on. The village squire would entertain his richer farmers and the farmer in turn would entertain his peers and those immediately beneath him. Nowhere do we find this process more admirably displayed than in Jane Austen's novels. Her precise portrayal of the 'upper middle class circle', the circle that touched the lower levels of nobility at its zenith and reached down to the soldier, merchant and poor curate at its nadir, is the most exact recreation of the pattern and process which dominated social activity in Georgian England. A process which, some would claim, averted the breakdown of government despite harsh inequalities and real adversity.

In this way 'the people' could have a voice and a place in English society. Handel had been much criticized for charging a guinea for admission to his opera *Deborah* for: 'Everybody knows that his Entertainments are calculated for the Quality only, and that People of moderate Fortunes cannot pretend to them.'

It is worth remembering that by contrast Haydn's very successful concerts in London were announced not only to nobility but *also* to gentlemen and their ladies. The pleasure gardens like Vauxhall, Ranelagh and those in Bath and Scarborough were places where the 'people of moderate Fortunes' were able to hear items by Purcell, Boyce and Arne under conditions that were geared to their modest 'wealth'. It was the same with many other things. Josiah Wedgwood boasted that not only did he make dinner services for the Csar of Russia, but also for the *people* of Britain. A certain butcher claimed that he did not fatten and slaughter his cattle to provide aristocrats with meat; but that he sought to *supply the public*. One startled nobleman exclaimed, there was no point in eating venison, if anyone could purchase it for their own table.

The pattern of exclusiveness and deprivation was to alter with the onset of mass-manufacture and good methods of retailing and supply. As with goods so it was with ideas. Circulating libraries and subscription lists for books accompany the growth of subscription concerts which in turn must be compared with the growth of shopping centres. We are fortunate to find that Jane Austen's letters chronicle the use that an upper middle class family made of these changes in social patterns.

The world of Jane Austen's novels is a microcosm illustrating the larger world beyond. She moves on the edges of nobility:

'Sir Walter Elliot, of Kellynch-hall, in Somersetshire, was a man who for his own amusement, never took up any book but the Baronetage; there he found occupation for an idle hour, and consolation in a distressed one . . .' [*Persuasion*, Vol III, Chapter I]

Through Mr Knightley in *Emma*, Jane Austen reflects upon our duties to those less fortunate than ourselves:

'"Emma, I must once more speak to you as I have been used to do: a privilege rather endured than allowed, perhaps, but I must still use it. I cannot see you acting wrong, without a remonstrance. How could you be unfeeling towards Miss Bates? How could you be so insolent in your wit to a woman of her character, age and situation? . . . . . . Were she a woman of fortune, I would leave every harmless absurdity to take its chance, I would not quarrel with you for any liberties of manner. Were she your equal in situation – but, Emma, consider how far this is from being the case. She is poor; she has sunk from the comforts she was born to; and if she live to an old age, must probably sink more. Her situation should secure your compassion . . ."' [Vol. III, Chapter VII]

Mr Knightley is forthright, and the social implications apt. The 'vertical' responsibility within the social circle is the one to which he refers *Emma* at this crucial moment in the novel.

Jane and Cassandra's friendships derive, naturally enough, from family connections. Their 'circle' was formed from the villages around Steventon on the one hand, and some of the great houses around Basingstoke, on the other. It was through the great estates, through the balls given at places like Hurstbourne, the family seat of Lord Portsmouth, that the Austen family 'reached' above their own social class. It was at the 'assemblies' in the town of Basingstoke that they mixed at more 'public' events. By joining in the social life of Hampshire, which was a society quite removed from royalty and the highest orders of nobility, the Austen family, and Jane Austen in particular, engaged in a more 'ordinary' social life, one that could be familiar to many of her readers.

With their friends, who were for the most part the sons, daughters, nephews and nieces of clergy, Jane and Cassandra explored all that there was for young ladies to enjoy in their immediate locality. They followed fashion, in dress, manners, music and behaviour. They went shopping, they indulged in gossip. Above all, as marriageable young women they whispered, and wrote letters about the young men with whom they allowed themselves to flirt in the ballroom, either in fact or in their fertile imaginations.

The Austen sisters paid many visits and in due course were much preoccupied, as is to be expected, with the young men whom they met while paying their 'social calls'.

The Angel, *Basingstoke, where the 'Basingstoke Assemblies' which Jane and Cassandra attended were held.*

Young Men and Women

OF THE FAMILIES with whom the Austens were friendly, three were very closely connected indeed. References to them feature more regularly than others and it is clear that much of Jane's and Cassandra's time was spent with these families. The families were the Lloyds, the Lefroys, and the Bigg-Withers. All three were to become connected 'romantically' and, in some cases, through marriage into the Austen family.

In the social hierarchy of Hampshire these families were very much in the same position as the Austens, a circle set out in the *Life* of Jane Austen published by her family:

'In the outer circle of their neighbourhood stood the houses of three peers–those of Lord Portsmouth at Hurstbourne, Lord Bolton of Hackwood and Lord Dorchester at Greywell. The owners of these places now and then gave balls at home, and could also be relied upon to bring parties to some of the assemblies at Basingstoke. Hardly less important than these magnates were the Mildmays of Dogsmersfield and the Chutes of the Vyne . . . then come the other squires–Portals at Freefolk, Bramstons at Oakley Hall, Jervoises at Herriard, Harwoods at Deane, Terrys at Dummer, Holders at Ashe Park–with several clerical families and other smaller folk.' [*Jane Austen, her Life and Letters* W. & R.A. Austen-Leigh, 1913]

The 'several clerical families' must include the Austens, the Lloyds and the Lefroys, who would meet at the occasional balls given in the great houses and at the more public assemblies in Basingstoke.

The Rev George Lefroy, parson at nearby Ashe, and his wife Anne, had considerable influence upon the Austen girls. Although she was twenty-five years older than Jane, Anne Lefroy became her very close friend, the young girl admiring the older woman almost to the point of adulation. Four years after her death (she was thrown from her horse on Jane Austen's twenty-ninth birthday), Jane composed a set of memorial verses which indicated her deep affection for Mrs Lefroy:

> *To the Memory of Mrs. Lefroy*
> The day returns again, my natal day!
>   What mix'd emotions in my mind arise!
> Beloved Friend; four years have passed away
>   Since thou wert snatched forever from our
>   eyes
> . . .
> Angelic woman! past my power to praise
>   In language meet thy talents, temper,
>   mind,
> Thy solid worth, thy captivating grace,
>   Thou friend and ornament of human kind.'

Thomas Lefroy, who came from one of the other parson families around Steventon, and who in old age confessed to having loved 'the great Jane Austen'.
J. G. Lefroy Esq.

But it was her nephew Thomas Lefroy who has interested biographers of Jane Austen most. For it is clear in the earliest surviving letter in Jane Austen's own hand that she had enjoyed that young man's company. Apart from the references to 'Tom Lefroy' this letter written at Steventon on Saturday 9th January 1796 tells us at once how the young men and women spent their time together and of the intimate relationship between Jane and her sister Cassandra:

In the first place I hope you will live twenty-three years longer. Mr. Tom Lefroy's birthday was yesterday, so that you are very near of an age.

After this necessary preamble I shall proceed to inform you that we had an exceeding good ball last night, and that I was very much disappointed at not seeing Charles Fowle of the party, as I had previously heard of his being invited . . .

We were so terrible good as to take James [her brother] in our carriage, though there were three of us before; but indeed he deserves encouragement for the very great improvement which has lately taken place in his dancing. Miss Heathcote is pretty, but not near so handsome as I expected. Mr. H. began with Elizabeth, and afterwards danced with her again; but *they* do not know how *to be particular*. I flatter myself, however, that they will profit by the three successive lessons which I have given them.

You scold me so much in the nice long letter which I have this moment received from you, that I am almost afraid to tell you how my Irish friend [Tom Lefroy] and I behaved. Imagine to yourself everything most profligate and shocking in the way of dancing and sitting down together.

On such evidence it has been argued that Jane and Thomas Lefroy were more to each other than merely dancing partners. He is the first of the eligible young men that tradition tells attracted Jane Austen. She continues to comment on him in her letter warning her sister that whatever relationship there is cannot last:

I *can* expose myself, however, only *once more*, because he leaves the country soon after next Friday, on which day we *are* to have a dance at Ashe after all. He is a very gentlemanlike, goodlooking, pleasant young man, I assure you. But as to our having ever met, except at the three last balls, I cannot say much; for he is so excessively laughed at about me at Ashe, that he is ashamed of coming to Steventon, and ran away when we called on Mrs Lefroy a few days ago.

A few tantalizing references in letters are all we really know of this early 'supposed' courtship. By the 16th January in the same year Jane was writing to tell Cassandra that Tom Lefroy would shortly be leaving for his native Ireland:

Friday. At length the day is come on which I am to flirt my last with Tom Lefroy, and when you receive this it will be over. My tears flow as I write at the melancholy idea.

Only Cassandra would know whether the tears really flowed; for most readers of Jane Austen, however, the claim has a satirical ring to it. However, Tom Lefroy did leave Hampshire, and was soon married in Ireland, where he became Lord Chief Justice. A passing reference to him in a letter some two years after the confession that she was to 'flirt her last', where she finds herself too proud to enquire after him, is all that there is about the man who in old age admitted that he once 'loved the great Jane Austen . . . but that it was a boy's love'. Perhaps the lost letters of 1796 to 1798 would tell us more of the man who for Jane Austen had but one fault: 'that his morning coat is a great deal too light'.

Morning carriage dress, from the ladies' periodical La Belle Assemblée. *Bath Reference Library.*

CASSANDRA

While we can only conjecture about Jane's attachment to Tom Lefroy we can be more sure of Cassandra's romance, for in 1796 Cassandra was engaged to be married. Her engagement, to the Rev Thomas Fowle, brought together two separate strands of the Hampshire social life. As a boy Thomas Fowle had been one of Cassandra's father's living-in pupils at Steventon Rectory, and later through the marriage of a brother he was connected with the Lloyds of Deane who were close friends of the Austens.

The widowed Mrs Lloyd and her daughters Martha, Eliza and Mary lived in George Austen's second parish of Deane, renting the unused parsonage. The Lloyd girls were such close friends of Jane and Cassandra that at one time they were to live with them. In time, both Martha and Mary were to marry Austen brothers. In 1796 Cassandra was staying with her fiancé's brother, Fulwer Craven Fowle, as her Thomas had set out to supplement his clergyman's stipend by serving as chaplain to Lord Craven's regiment in the West Indies. It was at this time that Jane had written her skittish letters about her 'flirtation' with Tom Lefroy.

Cassandra's engagement was doomed. The young clergyman fell sick of the yellow fever and died only a few weeks prior to his return to England. Eliza de La Feullide commented upon her cousin's grief:

Gillray here portrays the rebuff from the lady who does not wish to dance. A situation that Jane Austen knew in life and depicted in her novels.

This is a very severe stroke to the whole family, & particularly to poor Cassandra for whom I feel more than I can express. Indeed I am most sincerely grieved at this event & the pain which it must occasion our worthy relations. Jane says that her sister behaves with a degree of resolution & propriety which no common mind could evince in so trying a situation.

Although Cassandra was only twenty-four when her fiancé died, it appears that she never again contemplated marriage. No letters have survived that cover the exact period of Thomas Fowle's death; we may only guess the effect that such a shock would have upon a young woman preparing the clothes for her wedding.

Lord Craven, grieved at the news of the young man's death, vowed that he would not have let him go abroad had he known that he was engaged to be married.

Cassandra's engagement is the nearest that the Austen girls came to being married. Although known as 'two of the prettiest girls in England' and two of the most eligible they were to live as single women for the rest of their lives. In Cassandra's case this would be until she was seventy-two.

69

The house of 'Manydown' and the Bigg-Wither family that lived in it appear in Jane Austen's letters throughout her life. Clearly the daughters of this house, above all other, were the closest friends of the Austen girls. Elizabeth, Catherine and Althea Bigg formed parties with them to attend the balls at Basingstoke and to share the chatter and gossip that attended such functions.

Six miles from Steventon and near to Basingstoke, Manydown was the ideal setting for visiting. It was often the Austen girls' good fortune to stay in this large house in order to attend the balls given at Basingstoke as well as those given in Manydown itself. Our earliest surviving letter is an account of a Manydown ball, the very one where Jane 'flirted' with Tom Lefroy.

References to Manydown, to visits, to the people living there, span the years 1796 to 1813 in Jane Austen's letters. These references give us the clearest picture of the concerns of the young women in their leisure occupations. A typical letter to Cassandra describes a visit in 1798:

> I returned from Manydown this morning, and found my mother certainly in no respect worse than when I left her. She does not like the cold weather, but that we cannot help. I spent my time very quietly and very pleasantly with Catherine. Miss Blachford is agreeable enough. I do not want people to be very agreeable, as it saves me the trouble of liking them a great deal. I found only Catherine and her when I got to Manydown on Thursday. We dined together and went together to Worting to seek the protection of Mrs. Clarke, with whom were Lady Mildmay, her eldest son, and a Mr. & Mrs. Hoare.
>
> Our ball was very thin, but by no means unpleasant. There were thirty-one people, and only eleven ladies out of the number, and but five single women in the room. Of the gentlemen present you may have some idea from the list of my partners – Mr. Wood, G. Lefroy, Rice, a Mr. Butcher (belonging to the Temples, a sailor and not of the 11th Light Dragoons), Mr. Temple (not the horrid one of all), Mr. John Harewood, and Mr. Calland, who appeared as usual with his cap in his hand and stood every now and then behind Catherine and me to be talked to and abused for not dancing. We teased him, however, into it at last. I was very glad to see him again after so long a separation, and he was altogether rather the genius and flirt of the evening. He enquired after you.

A watercolour by Jane's sister Cassandra. None of Jane's own drawings or paintings survive though we are told that she was an accomplished draughtswoman and painter. T. E. Carpenter.

Fashion in the year 1797.

There were twenty dances, and I danced them all, and without any fatigue. I was glad to find myself capable of dancing so much, and with so much satisfaction as I did; from my slender enjoyment of the Ashford balls (as assemblies for dancing) I had not thought myself equal to it, but in cold weather and with few couples I fancy I could just as well dance for a week together as for half and hour. My black cap was openly admired by Mrs. Lefroy, and secretly I imagine by everybody else in the room.

[Letter to Cassandra, December 24, 1798]

From other letters we can build a picture of the young women enjoying themselves, appreciating the comfort of their surroundings, and taking not too solemn a view of life. As Jane was to write of a quiet evening spent with Mary Lloyd at Deane:

To sit in idleness over a good fire in a well-proportioned room is a luxurious sensation.

The letters referring to Manydown carry much about the society in which Jane Austen moved. We read of Harris Bigg-Wither's sudden illness, and of the 'two families of friends that are now in a most anxious state'. Harris Bigg-Wither's health seemed to be constant cause for alarm, while Earle Harewood, another dancing partner, had accidentally shot himself in the leg. This accident gives us a unique insight into the times in which these ladies were narrating their conquests:

Earle Harewood has been again giving uneasiness to his family, & Talk to the Neighbourhood; . . . –About ten days ago, in cocking his pistol in the guard room at Marcou, he accidentally shot himself through the Thigh. Two young Scotch Surgeons in the Island were polite enough to suggest taking off the Thigh at once, but to that he would not consent; and accordingly in his wounded state was put on board a Cutter and conveyed to Haslar Hospital at Gosport; where the bullet was extracted, & where he now is I hope in a fair way of doing well . . .

. . . *One* most material comfort however they have: the assurance of its being really an accidental wound, which is not only positively declared by Earle himself, but is likewise testified by the particular direction of the bullet. Such a wound could not have been received in a duel.

[Letter to Cassandra, 8 November 1800]

In 1801, again from Manydown, Jane writes to Cassandra, from the place where she tells her sister that she can expect 'Candour & Comfort & Coffee & Cribbage', to order material for dresses:

I shall want two new coloured gowns for the summer, for my pink one will not do more than clear me from Steventon. I shall not trouble you, however, to get more than one of them, and that is to be a plain brown cambris muslin, for morning wear; the other, which is to be a very pretty yellow and white cloud, I mean to buy in Bath . . .

. . . How do you like this cold weather? I hope you have all been earnestly praying for it as a salutary relief from the dreadfully mild and unhealthy season preceding it, fancying yourself half putrified from the want of it, and that now you all draw into the fire, complain that you never felt such bitterness of cold before, that you are half starved, quite frozen, and wish the mild weather back again with all your hearts.

[Letter to Cassandra, 25 January 1801]

Jane's last reference to Manydown is satirical:

I have been applied to for information as to the oath taken in former times of Bell, Book and Candle but have none to give. Perhaps you may be able to learn something of its origin and meaning at Manydown. Ladies who read those enormous great stupid thick quarto volumes which one always sees in the Breakfast parlour there, must be acquainted with everything in the world.

[Letter to Cassandra, 9 February 1813]

Long before this letter of 1813, however, events at Manydown had taken an unexpected turn, one which had caused Jane and Cassandra no little embarrassment. While they were both staying there in 1802 Harris Bigg-Wither had suddenly proposed to Jane and she had accepted him. Although he was a few years older than her it would have been a good match. Jane would marry into Hampshire society, she would 'be made' and would in time be able to provide for her mother and her sister. But after a sleepless night Jane reversed her decision at breakfast, gathered up her astonished sister and fled. We shall never know why Jane Austen accepted the proposal, nor why, after what must have been a tormenting night, she reversed her decision. Her constant advice to her nieces was that they should never marry where they did not "love". The "surprise" proposal may have produced a hasty "sensible" acceptance, the sense of which may have evaporated as the hours of the night passed. The story is told that Jane and Cassandra arrived at their brother's house in Steventon insisting that they must be returned at once to their home in Bath despite the short notice. And returned home they were. The experience left Jane somewhat uneasy with the Bigg-Wither connections, but it is clear that the friendship withstood the test and survived long after 1802.

The Novels in Solution

'I have in my possession a manuscript novel'

GEORGE and Cassandra Austen knew that their seventh child, their daughter Jane, was gifted. With the rest of the family they enjoyed her games with words and encouraged her precocious talent. In her more than in any other of the children they could see their own delight in literature reflected. At every stage of her development they supported and reinforced her exploration of words by example and interest. They more than tolerated her boisterous outbursts, they apparently positively encouraged them. George Austen was forty-four when Jane was born and the liveliness of the young girl's imagination must have appealed to him as he aged. Mrs Austen seems to have found her a handful judging by some of the comments she made from time to time. In a letter welcoming a daughter-in-law she permitted herself the following remark:

> Had the selection been mine, you my dear Mary, [Mary Lloyd, Jane's friend from Deane] are the person I should have chosen for James' wife, Anna's mother [Anna had been left motherless] and my daughter, being as certain as I can be of anything in this uncertain world, that you will greatly increase and promote the happiness of each of the three . . . I look forward to you as a real comfort to me in my old age when Cassandra is gone into Shropshire and Jane the Lord knows where.

Jane, who did not scruple to make the following entries in her father's registers at St Nicholas' church:

> Banns of Marriage:
> Henry Frederick Howard Fitzwilliam of London and Jane Austen of Steventon.
> Marriage:
> Jane Austen of Steventon to Arthur William Mortimer of Liverpool.

may well have left her mother wondering where she would end up. The delightfully naughty entries in the register are all of piece with the mock *History of England* and the parodying of pompous dedications in books.

George Austen's view of Jane's writing must have been kindly. We know that he provided her with books to write her stories down, an important practical help in the late eighteenth century when all writing materials were scarce and expensive. But he helped in other ways too. When Fanny Burney's *Camilla* was published in five volumes in 1796 we find the entry *Miss J. Austen, Steventon* in the list of subscribers to the edition. The family tradition claims that George Austen offered this appropriate present to Jane as encouragement. If so his thoughtfulness was more than amply rewarded.

From 1793, the date that is generally accepted for the completion of the last of the 'juvenile' pieces, until 1797, when we know that a three volume novel was complete in manuscript form, Jane Austen was continually at work. This was the period of reading and writing as much as of dancing and gossiping. The young women who made do with a put-you-up bed which 'did exceedingly well for us, both to lie awake in and talk till two o'clock, and to sleep in the rest of the night' could as easily have been telling stories as exchanging gossip about dancing partners. In *The Saturday Review* of 1884, there is a comment on her letters that suggests that however 'pretty' or 'silly' a 'husband-hunting butterfly' she might have been at this time, Jane Austen was living the life that she was so ably to recreate in her novels: 'The letters . . . contain . . . the matter of the novels in solution—in a very diluted, and not always a very unmixed, solution—but still there.' [Vol. 58, 15 November 1884]

The apparently 'trivial' world that so disappointed the readers of Jane Austen's letters must be seen as the seed-time of which the nicely observed scenes in the mature novels are the rich harvest. Visiting, receiving

Ladies observed frightening themselves with tales of wonder. This kind of story was very popular in the eighteenth century, and is cleverly satirized by Jane Austen in Northanger Abbey.

invitations, recounting ballroom escapades, the devising of strategies for the avoidance or acceptance of chaperones, all are indeed 'the novels in solution'. Armed with a keen eye and a sharp ear, the lady who was thrilled to start off the dancing in real life was also the lady who cherished the experience for what she could make of it in her imagination. The accuracy of her recreation of 'life' was no accident or extreme imaginative fancy. Jane Austen wrote of what she knew. The bonnets and the *bons mots* are the raw material of her art.

Jane Austen was undoubtedly an accomplished observer. It is said that on going to a concert she often chose to sit where she could watch the audience. From scenes like the following one in *Mansfield Park* we can believe this story.

Sir Thomas Bertram has suddenly returned to his home, where, without his knowledge, his billiard room has been turned into a theatre. Before anyone has a chance to prepare him for the news, he blunders onto the stage itself in the middle of a rehearsal. He passes through the door of his own room into what he thought was his billiard room:

'He stepped to the door . . . and opening it, found himself on the stage of a theatre, and opposed to a ranting young man, who appeared likely to knock him down backwards. At the very moment of Yates perceiving Sir Thomas, and giving perhaps the very best start he had given in the whole course of his rehearsals, Tom Bertram entered at the other end of the room; . . .' [Vol. II, Chapter I]

A few moments later the three gentlemen return to the drawing room, where the ladies are already gathered, and we can see how the 'very delicate' situation develops:

'"I come from your theatre," said he composedly, as he sat down; "I found myself in it rather unexpectedly. Its vicinity to my own room – but in every respect, indeed, it took me by surprise, as I had not the smallest suspicion of your acting having assumed so serious a character. It appears a neat job, however, as far as I could judge by candlelight . . ."

. . . And then he would have changed the subject, and

sipped his coffee in peace over domestic matters of a calmer hue; but Mr. Yates, without discernment to catch Sir Thomas's meaning, or diffidence, or delicacy, or discretion enough to allow him to lead the discourse . . . would keep him on the topic of the theatre, would torment him with questions and remarks relative to it . . .' [Ibid]

The scene is dramatically recreated, apparently without effort. It is not too far-fetched to say that it derives from the penetrating observation of the way people behave. We respond to the fiction because we recognize the truth it displays. Jane Austen must have been disarmingly perceptive with her own friends and those of the rest of her family. As the scene where the patient, though startled, Sir Thomas struggles to accommodate the unexpected addition to his home continues, Jane Austen's use of detail and unerring accuracy is magnificently displayed.

Mr Yates, shunning all attempts to tread softly, blunders on:

'Mr. Yates took the subject from his friend as soon as possible, and immediately gave Sir Thomas an account of what they had done and were doing; told him of the gradual increase of their views, the happy conclusion of their first difficulties, and present promising state of affairs; relating everything with so blind an interest as made him not only totally unconscious of the uneasy movements of many of his friends as they sat, the change of countenance, the fidget, the hem! of unquietness, but

Ladies at a pianoforte. Jane Austen owned an instrument of this kind which, it is said, she would play before breakfast and in private.

prevented him even from seeing the expression of the face on which his own eyes were fixed—from seeing Sir Thomas's dark brow contract as he looked with enquiring earnestness at his daughters and Edmund, dwelling particularly on the latter, and speaking a language, a remonstrance, a reproof, which *he* felt at his heart.' [Ibid]

Amateur theatricals at Steventon are an obvious source for much of this section of *Mansfield Park*. The uncomfortably accurate picture of insensitivity must derive also from amused but penetrating observation. Mr Yates's lack of delicacy, his blundering insensitivity, and Sir Thomas's smouldering anger all derive from the kind of situation that Jane and Cassandra would know well. From Jane's letters we can trace the source of many of her scenes:

Charles [Jane's younger brother] is not come yet, but he must come this morning, or he shall never know what I will do to him. The ball at Kempshott is this evening, and I have got him an invitation, though I have not been so considerate as to get him a partner. But the cases are different between him and Eliza Bailey, for he is not in a dying way, and may therefore be equal to getting a partner for himself. I believe I told you that Monday was to be the ball night, for which and for all other errors into which I may have led you, I humbly ask your pardon.'
[Letter to Cassandra, 8 January 1799]

A long letter to Cassandra written in November, 1800 is a *tour de force* of brisk devastating description:

Your letter took me quite by surprise this morning; you are very welcome, however, and I am very much obliged to you.—I believe I drank too much wine last night at Hurstbourne; [home of Lord Portsmouth] I know not how else to account for the shaking of my hand today;—You will kindly make allowance therefore for any indistinctness of writing by attributing it to this venial Error . . .

. . . There were very few Beauties, & such as there were, were not very handsome . . . Mrs. Blount was the only one much admired. She appeared exactly as she did in September, with the same broad face, diamond bandeau, white shoes, pink husband and fat neck . . . The Miss Maitlands are both prettyish . . . with brown skins, large dark eyes, & a good deal of nose.—

. . . We had a very pleasant day on Monday at Ashe . . . Mrs. Bramston talked a good deal of nonsense which Mr. Bramston & Mr. Clerk seemed almost equally to enjoy.—there was a

whist & a casino table, & six outsiders. – Rice and Lucy made love, Mat. Robinson fell asleep, James and Mrs. Augusta alternately read Dr. Jenner's pamphlet on the cow pox, and I bestowed my company by turns on them all.

[Letter to Cassandra, 20 November 1800]

Jane Austen was a practised reporter. She was quick to notice things and adroit in recreating scenes and conveying atmosphere. Her letters are for a writer what the many pencil sketches are for painters: the jottings and shorthand versions of character, event, situations and feelings. Her experiences in her social environment gave her many opportunities to notice behaviour: her informal writing offered an equal chance to capture those experiences in their retelling.

It is perhaps worth pausing to notice how elegantly, in the opening of this letter, Jane Austen is able to admit to having a hangover.

But experience is one thing, weaving stories from that experience quite another. Alongside the opportunity to mix in society a young writer needs to refine his talent. In Jane Austen's case, as with so many other writers, the apprenticeship was served in reading.

It is not surprising to find that the home of the Rev George Austen, a one-time fellow of an Oxford college, was filled with books. We are wrong, however, if we imagine that his library was purely theological. The

A contemporary depiction of a situation common in Jane's novels: a young lady tries to 'catch' a young man by the power of her musical accomplishments.

books at Steventon were not all sermons, and Jane writes to Cassandra in 1798:

I have received a very civil note from Mrs. Martin requesting my name as a Subscriber to her Library which opens the 14th of January, & my name, or rather Yours, is accordingly given. My Mother finds the Money. – Mary subscribes too, which I am glad of, but hardly expected. – As an inducement to subscribe Mrs. Martin tells us that her Collection is not to consist only of Novels, but of every kind of Literature, etc, etc – She might have spared this pretension to *our* family, who are great Novel-readers and not ashamed of being so;

. . .

[Letter to Cassandra, 18 December 1798]

The reading of the Austen family was wide-ranging, the list of books mentioned in Jane's letters impressive in quantity and variety: books as diverse as Shakespeare and *An Essay on the Military Police*. All kinds of books, from the classics to the latest piece of romantic fiction, appear in the reading lists and correspondence of the Austen household. Richardson, Johnson, Cowper (a special favourite), Boswell and Fielding were available

A circulating library, referred to in Jane Austen's
novels and used by her in life. It was these libraries
that ensured novelists a market.

to Jane, as well as Thomas Gisborne's *Enquiry into the Duties of the Female Sex*; William Godwin and Jenner as well as Charlotte Lennox's *The Female Quixote, or The Adventures of Isabella*.

Jane Austen's lack of shame at her family's delight in novels is significant. Not everyone would be so confident. A former headmaster of Tonbridge School, where George Austen was both a pupil and a schoolmaster, Vicessimus Knox, spoke for many when he laid the blame for current immorality at the novelists' feet: 'If it be true that the present age is more corrupt than the preceding, the great multiplication of Novels has probably contributed to its degeneracy'. What Knox feared was the lowering of standards as literature depicted habits and ways which were not always good examples, stories where he feared that 'A softened appellation has given a degree of gracefulness to moral deformity'. It is interesting to reflect that a daughter of a former pupil and second master of Knox's school would do more for the popularity of the novel in English than many other writers of that century.

By November 1st 1797 George Austen was confident that Jane was a writer. After the readings to the family and the general agreement that his daughter's work was enjoyable he wrote to a London publisher:

Sir,

I have in my possession a manuscript novel, comprising 3 vols., about the length of Miss Burney's Evelina. As I am well aware of what consequence it is that a work of this sort should make its first appearance under a respectable name, I apply to you. I shall be much obliged therefore if you will inform me whether you choose to be concerned in it, what will be the expense of publishing it at the author's risk, and what you will venture to advance for the property of it, if on perusal it is approved of. Should you give any encouragement, I will send you the work.

I am, Sir, your humble servant,
George Austen.

The publisher, Cadell, declined, and we hear no more of attempts to have the novel, known in the family as *First Impressions*, published for a good few years.

Jane Austen refers to this novel twice in the letters which have survived. In the first case she is gently chiding Cassandra:

I do not wonder at your wanting to read 'First Impressions' again, so seldom as you have gone through it, and that so long ago.
[Letter to Cassandra, 8 January 1799]

In June of the same year Jane teases:

I would not let Martha (Lloyd) read 'First Impressions' again on any account, and am

76

very glad that I did not leave it in your power. She is very cunning, but I saw through her design; she means to publish it from memory, and one more perusal must enable her to do it. [Letter to Cassandra, 11 June 1799]

No copy of *First Impressions* has survived. But years later in 1813, after the successful sales of *Sense and Sensibility*, it was re-written, or 'lop't and crop't' as Jane Austen called it, to be published as *Pride and Prejudice*.

We cannot be certain of the form of this early novel. Some believe that it was written in the convention of the novel in letter form, others that Jane Austen was already using a third person narrative. Whatever might be the truth it is worth considering the kinds of novel that were currently available at the time *First Impressions* was being written.

In the late eighteenth century it was still rather unusual for women to write novels. Hence George Austen's guarded letter and the need for Jane Austen to publish anonymously. Being a novelist, and a lady novelist, was not altogether comfortable. Fanny Burney, who could shelter beneath the august patronage of Dr Johnson, is quite clear about this:

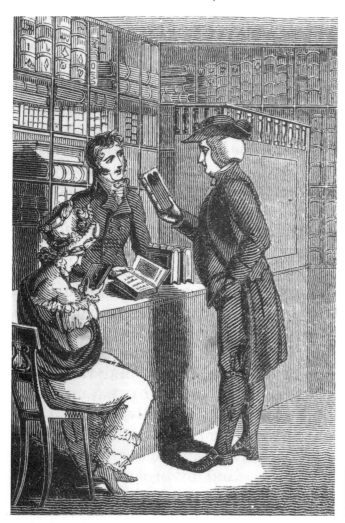

A bookseller's shop.

'In the republic of letters, there is no member of such inferior rank, or who is so much disdained by his brethren of the quill, as the humble novelist . . .'
In the preface to *Evelina* she comments upon the advisability of being 'happily wrapped up in a mantle of impenetrable obscurity'.

A glance at some of the comments aimed at young ladies about the inadvisability of *reading* novels might serve to indicate how dangerous it could be thought to actually *write* them:
'Novels inflame the passions of youth, whilst the chief purpose of education should be to moderate and restrain them.'
'The expectation of extraordinary adventures–which seldom happen to the sober and prudent part of mankind–and the admiration of extravagant passions and absurd conduct, are some of the usual fruits of this kind of reading; which when a young woman makes it her chief amusement, generally renders her ridiculous in conversation, and miserably wrong-headed in her pursuits and behaviour.' [*Letters on the Improvement of the Mind*, Mrs Chapone]
Such a 'precious' view of young ladies was one that Jane Austen could not abide. It was her purpose to lampoon such repressive views, and there were many such expressed in her day, whenever she could in her writing. The most telling attack upon such attitudes comes in one of her minor works, in a piece entitled:
A Letter from a Young Lady, whose feelings being too strong for her Judgement led her into the commission of Errors which her Heart disapproved.
'Many have been the cares and vicissitudes of my past life, my beloved Ellinor, & the only consolation I feel for their bitterness is that on a close examination of my conduct, I am convinced that I have strictly deserved them. I murdered my father at a very early period of my Life, I have since murdered my Mother, and I am now going to murder my Sister. I have changed my religion so often that at present I have no idea of any left. I have been a perjured witness at every public tryal for these last twelve years; and I have forged my own will. In short there is scarcely a crime that I have not committed.' [*Scraps*, from *Volume the Second*]

Jane Austen was forthright in her condemnation of the pious sermons in moralizing writing. She was equally scornful of the extravagant 'Gothic' tales. A review in *The Gentleman's Magazine* of the state of the novel in the eighteenth century pinpoints that form of excess which together with the romantic fantasies Jane Austen was so determined to avoid:
'The wonderful and miraculous is the *forte* of our modern novel writers. Instead of pictures drawn from life, 'catching the Manners living as they rise', we have narrations of haunted towers, old Bluebeards and Redbeards, spectres, sprites, apparitions, black banners

waving on battlements of castles, strange voices, tapers burning one moment and extinguished by some unknown hand the next, clandestine noises, flashings of lightning, and howling of winds.'

We can appreciate Sir Walter Scott's delight with Jane Austen when he found that her characters were indeed 'drawn from life' and that she only resorted to heroines who were 'faultless monsters that the world ne'er saw', when she was in a satirical mood. We only have to turn to *Northanger Abbey* to see how she disposes of the 'Gothic Tale'.

Mr Tilney, in taking the heroine Catherine to visit his home for the first time, allows himself to tease her about Northanger Abbey, and modern fiction at the same time:

'". . . you will proceed into this small vaulted room, and through this into several others, without perceiving anything remarkable in either. In one, perhaps, there might be a dagger, in another, a few drops of blood, and in a third the remains of some instrument of torture; but there being nothing in all this out of the common way, and your lamp being nearly exhausted, you will return towards your own apartment . . .' [Vol II, Chapter VI]

The manuscript that Jane's father 'had in his possession' was an unusual one in its day. It was not a moral tale for young ladies, neither was it the escapist fantasy of romantic fiction. If it was an early version of *Pride and Prejudice* it fulfilled Richard Cumberland's criteria for a novel, criteria that he was to declare in 1795, just two years before Jane's father offered the manuscript of *First Impressions* to Cadell:

'An author will naturally cast his composition in that kind of style and character where he thinks himself most likely to succeed; and in this he will be directed by considering, in the first place, what is the natural turn of his own mind, where his strength lies, and to what his talents point; and secondly to the public taste, which, however much it is his interest to consult, should not be suffered to betray him into undertakings he is not fitted for.'

No author more aptly fits Cumberland's definition than Jane Austen. She never wrote beyond her scope, and she firmly refused every invitation and temptation to write of anything other than what came naturally to her mind.

Although George Austen's letter to Cadell was unsuccessful it marks an important step in Jane Austen's writing career. For the first time (to our knowledge) she and her family were looking beyond their own delight and amusement in her work. Whatever *First Impressions* might have been its having been offered to a London Publisher should once and for all refute the claim that Jane Austen only wrote to amuse her family. It is not possible that her father should write to Cadell without her knowledge, nor should we believe that she would be reluctant to see her work in print. Her excitement and delight over the publication of *Sense and Sensibility* in 1811 confirms her quite normal enjoyment of authorship.

There must have been some disappointment at Steventon when Cadell declined to show any interest in the offered manuscript. But there is nothing to suggest that Jane Austen was deterred from continuing to write, quite the contrary in fact. By 1803 another novel *Susan* was ready to be sent to a publisher, but not before the Austen family had left Steventon to live in Bath.

Bath

'Disordering my Stomach with Bath Bunns'

JANE AUSTEN knew all the delights of Bath well before she went to live there on her father's retirement in 1801. From *Northanger Abbey* and *Persuasion* we can be certain of her intimate and detailed knowledge of the customs, entertainments and advantages of the famous watering place as well as of its street plan. It is possible to trace the footsteps in present day Bath of Anne Elliot and Catherine Morland, and visitors today can admire views that are little changed since 1800 and may still 'disorder' their stomachs with 'Bath Bunns'.

But while Jane Austen may jest about her diet, she was not at all amused with the prospect of leaving Hampshire and her beloved Steventon for the much praised elegance of Bath. Her niece, Caroline Austen, writing to her brother in 1869, recalled how:

> My Aunt was very sorry to leave her native home, as I have heard my Mother relate. My Aunts had been away a little while, and were met in the Hall on their return by their Mother who told them it was all settled, and they were going to live in Bath. My Mother who was present said my Aunt was greatly distressed. All things were done in a hurry by Mr. Austen.

Other more alarming accounts tell us that Jane Austen fainted. Whether or not she emulated one of her own heroines at a time of stress or not we can be sure that the move would not have pleased her. For twenty-five years she had lived extremely happily in the country. From Steventon she had been able to make shopping forays into Basingstoke or even as far as London, but she had always relished her return to the tree-lined walks and serenity of the Hampshire countryside. In time, however, she became reconciled to the move:

> I get more and more reconciled to the idea of our removal. We have lived long enough in this neighbourhood, the Basingstoke Balls are

A typical Bath street, showing the good town planning with both wide streets for carriages and good pavements for pedestrians.

certainly on the decline, there is something interesting in the bustle of going away, and the prospect of spending future summers by the Sea or in Wales is very delightful. – For a time we shall now possess many of the advantages which I have often thought of with Envy in the wives of Sailors or Soldiers. – It must not be known however that I am not sacrificing a great deal in quitting the Country – or I can expect to inspire no tenderness, no interest in those we leave behind.

[Letter to Cassandra, 3 January 1801]

The astute reader of Jane Austen's novels and letters may discern a touch of irony in her professed reconciled contentment. It is by no means clear that Jane ever really delighted in living in Bath. The reasons for this may be found in a careful examination of just what the move from Steventon to Bath implied. Beyond the selling of the library of over 500 books, of the furniture (it was not worth the inconvenience of trying to transport it), of Jane's pianoforte, there was the leaving of her mother's farm and the abrupt and lasting severance from a totally rural setting. The Austen family's destination was by no means merely another house in a different place. Life at Bath was a highly sophisticated activity in a specially built town.

By the time that the Austens went to live there, Bath was a town of some 30,000 inhabitants, who either lived in luxury themselves or administered the luxuries that were offered for the minority who could afford them. The population of the fashionable watering place, a place of splendour and ease, equalled that of industrial Leeds at the turn of the nineteenth century. Of all the watering places in England Bath was not only the most popular; it was also the most highly developed in every way.

Bath's popularity derived from the medicinal qualities of the waters found there, but more significantly from Queen Anne's visits in 1701 and 1702. The entertainments at that time were so lavish and so successful that the post of Master of Ceremonies remained after the Queen had left. The city, which had previously catered for the sick, found itself catering for visitors on a grand scale. The development of Bath into a major eighteenth-century 'industry' or enterprise can be traced to the work of three or four men: Ralph Allen, John Wood and his son, and Masters of Ceremony like Beau Nash. The businessmen and the Masters of Ceremony combined their efforts to make Bath a worthy setting for the richest of visitors. Allen was the businessman behind the enterprise, the Woods were the builders. Together they created a city that remains something of a wonder.

The Pump Room, Bath. Sedan chairs and the 'Pump Room' indicate the 'double life' of the Spa. Visitors came for a 'cure' and the town lived off the visitors, often charging inflated prices as part of a 'luxury trade' founded upon ill-health and poor medical knowledge. Victoria Art Gallery, Bath.

Bath was continuously and brilliantly developed throughout the eighteenth century, so that the Bath Jane Austen knew was in a great part newly built. Ironically its popularity in her lifetime was to wane as sea-bathing and the Prince Regent's enjoyment of Brighton increased.

The move from Steventon, from the small farm, the secluded lanes and the tiny village church, was a move to a busy and highly 'tuned' place of fashionable indulgence filled with bustle, inflated prices and all the trappings of the 'entertainment business' in the far from fastidious eighteenth century. From the house that had its own elm trees, a sloping lawn, a shaded walk and a sweep to the front door, Jane Austen was to move to a town house or apartment where all the necessaries of life would have to be purchased from tradesmen. A town apartment is a far cry from a country rectory with its own herd of cows.

The shock would be softened for Jane Austen however because she had already visited Bath and stayed there from time to time. Her grandmother Mrs Thomas Leigh had lived in Bath and her only son James Leigh, who adopted the name Leigh Perrot, had lived there since 1768. Uncle James and Aunt Jane Leigh Perrot figure frequently in Jane Austen's letters and we have evidence that Jane and her mother stayed in Bath before 1801.

Rowlandson's cartoon of the interior of the Pump Room

Richard. (Beau) Nash (1674-1762) whose skill as a master of ceremonies matched the abilities of the John Woods and of Ralph Allen in their building of Bath. Beau Nash founded the traditions that society observed at the resort, inventing a way of life for those who came to the spa, and the whole mode of fashionable life that was to last to parody. National Portrait Gallery, London.

Bath was an exciting place for a young woman, as after London it had the most elaborate pattern of entertainments and social activities. Here the most fashionable clothes could be seen, and the most elegant people observed. For through the efforts of Beau Nash and other Masters of Ceremonies, the visitors to Bath were made into a community with its own code of conduct, its courtesies, its privileges and its particular round of social events. All this needed a setting and one that was devoted to pleasure. Bath was a brilliant solution to the problem. The opportunity to develop a city as a leisure centre was seized and the enterprise was a notable success in Europe as well as in England. Jane Austen's arrival late in the day, for Bath had past its zenith by 1801, was to ensure the city's place in literary as much as in architectural and social history. *Northanger Abbey* and *Persuasion,* with their detailed descriptions of the place and the social conventions observed, tell us of Bath and its former glory more effectively than any guide book.

Fortunately for us, Joseph Haydn, on his second concert tour in London, visited Bath in 1794 and wrote in some detail of what he found:
'On 2nd August 1794, I left at 5 o'clock in the morning for Bath, with Mr. Ashe and Mr. Cimador, and arrived there at 8 o'clock in the evening. It's 107 miles from

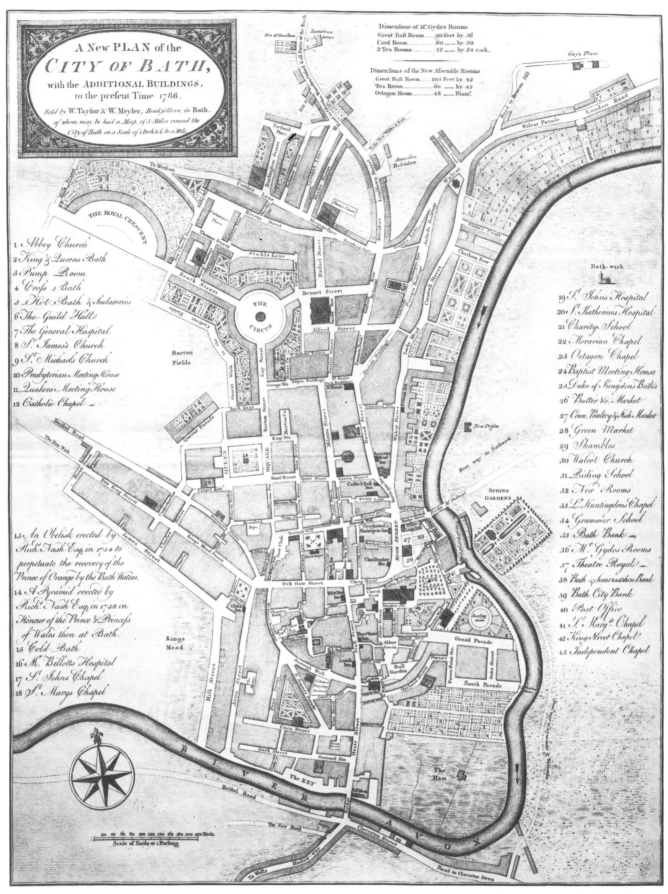

Dimensions of M^r. Gyde's Rooms
Great Ball Room .... 90 Feet by 36
Card Room .... 60 ____ by 30
2 Tea Rooms .... 42 ____ by 24 each.

Dimensions of the New Assembly Rooms
Great Ball Room ...... 105 Feet by 42
Tea Room .... 60 ____ by 42
Octagon Room .... 48 ____ Diam^t.

A New PLAN of the
CITY OF BATH,
with the ADDITIONAL BUILDINGS,
to the present Time 1786.

Sold by W. Taylor & W. Meyler, Booksellers, in Bath.
of whom may be had a Map, of 5 Miles round the
City of Bath on a Scale of 1 Inch & 1/4 to a Mile.

1. Abbey Church
2. King & Queens Bath
3. Pump Room
4. Cross Bath
5. Hot Bath & Sudatories
6. The Guild Hall
7. The General Hospital
8. St James's Church
9. St Michaels Church
10. Presbyterian Meeting House
11. Quakers Meeting House
12. Catholic Chapel

13. An Obelisk erected by
Rich^d. Nash Esq. in 1734 to
perpetuate the recovery of the
Prince of Orange by the Bath Waters.
14. A Pyramid erected by
Rich^d. Nash Esq. in 1738 in
Honour of the Prince & Princess
of Wales then at Bath.
15. Cold Bath
16. M^r. Bellotts Hospital
17. St Johns Chapel
18. St Marys Chapel

19. St Johns Hospital
20. St Katherines Hospital
21. Charity School
22. Moravian Chapel
23. Octagon Chapel
24. Baptist Meeting House
25. Duke of Kingstons Baths
26. Butter &c. Market
27. Corn, Poultry & Fish Market
28. Green Market
29. Shambles
30. Walcot Church
31. Riding School
32. New Rooms
33. L^y Huntingdons Chapel
34. Grammar School
35. Bath Bank
36. M^r. Gydes Rooms
37. Theatre Royal
38. Bath & Somersetshire Bank
39. Bath City Bank
40. Post Office
41. St Mary^s Chapel
42. King Street Chapel
43. Independent Chapel

An eighteenth-century plan of Bath, showing many of the streets mentioned in Persuasion *and* Northanger Abbey. *Jane Austen's use of Bath in her novels is careful and accurate. We can trace the paths of her heroines as they shop or promenade in the hope of meeting or avoiding 'certain' gentlemen. Victoria Art Gallery, Bath.*

An aerial view of twentieth-century Bath. The elegant streets can still be seen. John Wood (the elder) built the Circus, while his son John Wood (the second) built the impressive Royal Crescent. Between them, father and son were responsible for developing a city that was renowned throughout Europe for its elegance, an elegance which it still preserves today.

London. The Mail Coach does this distance in 12 hours . . .

. . . Bath is one of the most beautiful cities in Europe. All the houses are built of stone; this stone comes from quarries in the surrounding mountains; it is very soft, so soft, in fact, that it's no trouble to cut it up into any desired shape; it is very white, and the older it is, once it has been taken from the quarry, the harder it gets. The whole city lies on a slope, and that is why there are few carriages; instead of them, there are a lot of sedan-chairs, who will take you quite a way for 6 pence. But too bad there are so few straight roads; there are a lot of beautiful squares, on which stand the most magnificent houses, but which cannot be reached by any vehicle: they are now building a brand new and broad street.'

Haydn described many of Bath's outstanding features, but failed to realize that the whole was designed for the pedestrian. The pavements set high above the road made it possible for fashionably dressed men and women to promenade away from the bustle and hurly-burly of wheeled transport. The Circus and the Crescent were specifically designed so that wheeled transport could not get to them in the same way as to ordinary streets or squares. With its pavements and overall planning Bath was far in advance of any other city both socially and architecturally.

Other visitors have also left their impressions of Bath. In 1732 Macky published the following account in his *Journey Through England:*

Above: Town and Country meet in this Rowlandson
cartoon entitled **Bath Beau and Country Beau**.
*The health of the latter is contrasted with the langours
of the fashionable young men of Bath. The contrast
must have been one that Jane Austen felt sharply when
she moved from rural Hampshire to live in an apartment
in the fashionable city. Birmingham City Art Gallery.*

Below: The Upper Assembly Rooms, Bath, from a
painting by Thomas Malton in 1790. It is the scene
of the balls and assemblies that Jane herself attended
and the scenario for many incidents in her novels. By
the time that Jane came to live in Bath its popularity
was already in decline, its glories beginning to fade.
Laing Art Gallery, Newcastle on Tyne.

Paragon Buildings, Bath, where Jane stayed with her aunt, Mrs Perrot, but where she and her mother declined to live when they retired to Bath. Bath Reference Library.

'Bath lies very low; it is but a small city, but very compact; and one can hardly imagine it could accommodate near the Company that frequents it, at least three Parts of the year. I have been told of 8,000 families there at a time, some for the Benefit of drinking its hot Waters, others for Bathing, and others for Diversion and Pleasure; of which I must say, it affords more than any public place of its kind in *Europe* . . . Here Visits are received and returned, Assemblies and Balls are given, and Parties at Play in most Houses every night.'

Pierce Egan, in his *Walks through Bath*, completes the picture:

'All is bustle and gaiety; numerous dashing equipages passing and repassing, others gracing the doors of the tradesmen; sprinkled here and there with invalids in comfortable Sedans and easy two wheeled carriages, all anxious to participate in this active part of Bath, giving a sort of finish to the scene . . . in short Milsom and Bond Streets afford to the utmost extent towards supplying the real or imaginary wants of the visitors: containing libraries to improve the mind, musical repositories to enrich their taste and science, confectioners to invite the most fastidious appetite, tailors, milliners, etc., of the highest eminence in the fashionable world.'

The move from the country to the city amplified Jane Austen's artistic vision at the same time as it changed her life-style. She may never have felt at home in Bath, and she spoke of her departure in clearly unfavourable terms:

It will be two years tomorrow since we left Bath for Clifton, with what happy feelings of Escape.
[Letter to Cassandra, 30 June 1808]

But as her first novel, *Northanger Abbey*, and her last, *Persuasion*, were both set in Bath, and both draw upon the conventions of Bath society, it cannot be convincingly argued that she either stopped writing or failed to make use of the environment in which she found herself. On the contrary the scenes in Bath complement, if not rather tellingly juxtapose, the scenes in the country houses which we find as major settings for her action. Sir Walter Elliot in *Persuasion* provides an example of the use Jane Austen made of living in the prime resort in England:

'Sir Walter thought much of Mrs. Wallis; she was said to be an excessively pretty woman, beautiful. "He longed to see her. He hoped she might make amends for the many very plain faces he was continually passing in the

The Royal Crescent, Bath, in a painting by Watts that shows the wide pavement and the overall design that so characterized the Woods' development of Bath, the paved streets being something of an innovation. Victoria Art Gallery, Bath.

streets. The worst of Bath was, the number of plain women. He did not mean to say that there were no pretty women, but the number of plain was out of all proportion. He had frequently observed, as he walked, that one handsome face would be followed by thirty, or five and thirty frights; and once, as he had stood in a shop in Bond-street, he had counted eighty-seven women go by, one after another, without there being a tolerable face among them. It had been a frosty morning, to be sure, a sharp frost, which hardly one woman in a thousand could stand the test of. But still, there certainly were a dreadful multitude of ugly women in Bath; and as for men! they were infinitely worse. Such scare-crows as the streets were full of! It was evident how little the women were used to the sight of anything tolerable, by the effect which a man of decent appearance produced. He had never walked anywhere arm in arm with Colonel Wallis, (who was a fine military figure, though sandy-haired) without observ-

ing that every women's eye was upon him; every woman's eye was sure to be upon Colonel Wallis.''' [Vol. IV, Chapter III]

One could not imagine standing in such a shop in the village of Steventon and five and thirty faces might be as many as one would see in a week in the lonely lanes of Hampshire.

Jane Austen married her familiarity with the country with her knowledge of the city. Her country houses and their upper middle class inhabitants complement the apartments of Bath with their elegant seasonal occupants. If the time spent in Bath was one of revision, and not creative story-writing, as many believe, it was without any doubt a period of observation and a broadening experience which Jane Austen was to exploit fully in her work. We have too readily accepted her advice to her niece as descriptive of her work:

. . . three or four Families in a Country Village is the very thing to work on

[Letter to Anna Austen, 9 September 1814]

Her own fictitious families *do not* stay in villages, nor do they only inhabit country houses. The bustle of Bath is used as a counterpoise to life elsewhere. Jane Austen was quite capable of exploiting any setting that she wished. The unfinished work known as *Sanditon* convincingly

demonstrates her ability to create a setting and to use it. Sanditon is a growing seaside resort and this working draft of a novel shows Jane Austen working in a different key. The scenes set in Lyme Regis, as well as those in Bath and Sanditon, amply confirm her ability to set the people that she knows well in places that suit her artistic needs. Moreover, it is worth noticing that *Sanditon* was the novel that she was working on when she died, and it is significant that she had moved her *dramatis personae* to a seaside town. With her zeal for accuracy and concern to write of the *present* preoccupations of the world in which she lived she was consciously seeking to be topical–always the hallmark of a good novelist.

Jane Austen knew that novels needed to be up to date. Her apology in the front of *Northanger Abbey* (her first 'Bath' novel) is unequivocal:

Advertisement by the Authoress

This little work was finished in the year 1803, and intended for immediate publication. It was disposed of to a bookseller, it was even advertised, and why the business proceeded no farther, the author has never been able to learn. That any bookseller should think it worth while to purchase what he did not think it worth while to publish seems extraordinary. But with this, neither the author nor the public have any other

The Royal Crescent, Bath, as it is in the twentieth century, little changed even today as a piece of boldly designed architecture well executed.

concern than as some observation is necessary upon those parts of the work which thirteen years have made completely obsolete. The public are entreated to bear in mind that thirteen years have passed since it was finished, many more since it was begun, and that during that period, places, manners, books, and opinions have undergone considerable changes.'

From so frank a statement we can confidently infer that during those thirteen years Miss Austen's knowledge of 'the places, manners, books, and opinions' had kept pace with the changes. Jane Austen was fiercely critical of inaccuracy and took a pride in being topical. A single example from *Sanditon* serves to show at once her economy and social 'precision'. Here Mr Parker is waxing eloquent about the advantages of his new house, in itself a comment upon the need to 'improve' upon the past (an abiding eighteenth-century concern):

'"This is my old house–the house of my forefathers . . . one other hill brings us to Sanditon–modern Sanditon–a beautiful spot.–Our ancestors you know always built in a hole. Here were we, pent down in this

87

little contracted nook, without air in view, only a mile and three quarters from the noblest expanse of ocean between the south foreland and the land's end, and without the smallest advantage from it. You will not think I have made a bad exchange, when we reach Trafalgar House–which by the bye, I almost wish I had not named Trafalgar–for Waterloo is ,more the thing now. However Waterloo is in reserve–and if we have encouragement enough this year for a little crescent to be ventured on–(as I trust we shall) then, we shall be able to call it Waterloo Crescent–and then the name joined to the form of the building, which always takes, will give us a command of lodgers–. In a good season we should have more applications than we could attend to."' [Chapter IV]

'Waterloo is more the thing now' and Jane Austen was very much aware that novels are concerned with such changes in fashion. The seaside town of Sanditon is clearly developing, at least in Mr Parker's eyes, along the lines of Bath or Brighton. With its crescent, its visitors and its subscription library *Sanditon* could be seen as Mr Parker's Bath, with Mr Parker playing the part of Allen and Wood who developed the real resort of Bath so successfully.

Bath brought the art of the picturesque into a city: as gardens had been landscaped and planned to please the eye, so the buildings and amenities of the developing city were part of an overall scheme. Jane Austen, on one of her earliest recorded visits, describes the view from her apartment window:

> The prospect from the drawing room window,
> at which I now write, is rather picturesque, as
> it commands a perspective view of the left side
> of Brook Street, broken by three Lombardy
> poplars in the garden of the last house in
> Queen's Parade.
> [Letter to Cassandra, 17 May 1799]

Jane Austen had much to say about the picturesque, and much to write of what she viewed from her window during the years that she spent in Bath.

Queen's Square in the eighteenth century. Bath was designed with pedestrians in mind, hence the sedan chairs and the paved areas which formed early pedestrian precincts.

1801 to 1806

JANE AUSTEN's arrival in Bath in 1801 did not inspire her:

> The first view of Bath in fine weather does not answer my expectations; I think I see more distinctly through rain. The sun gets behind everything, and the appearance of the place from the top of Kingsdown was all vapour, shadow, smoke, and confusion.
> [Letter to Cassandra, 5 May 1801]

Her journey there she considered uneventful:

> Our journey here was perfectly free from accident or event; we changed horses at the end of every stage, and paid at almost every turnpike. We had charming weather, hardly any dust, and were exceedingly agreeable, as we did not speak above once in three miles.
> [Ibid]

The wry comment at the end of this paragraph typifies the twenty-six-year-old woman's attitude to most things while she lived in Bath. The five years there were to be disappointing. They were years when she rewrote an earlier novel, failed once again to have her writing published, and during the course of which her father died at the age of seventy-four. Moreover, amidst the splendours of Bath, splendours which she could at times enjoy, Jane Austen was at all times in subordinate, dependent circumstances. As an unmarried woman she lived with her parents and moved in their circle. A circle of aunts and uncles, of polite visiting and reliance upon somebody else's carriage for transport. The many letters to her sister Cassandra tell of small parties, of dinners and tea parties as often as they describe entertainments in the Sydney Gardens, the pleasure gardens or the theatre. Life with a retired clergyman in his seventies would necessarily be rather sedate, and it is therefore not surprising to find that letters take a domestic tone in this period:

> I am not without hopes of tempting Mrs. Lloyd to settle in Bath; meat is only 8d per pound, butter 12d, and cheese $9\frac{1}{2}$d. You must carefully conceal from her, however, the price of fish; a salmon has been sold at 2s 9d per pound the whole fish. The Duchess of York's removal is expected to make that article more reasonable–and till it really appears so, say nothing about salmon.
> [Ibid]

The inflated price caused by the Duchess's visit to Bath betrays something of the nature of the city's business foundations. The exploitation of visitors and other customers that was commonplace in towns and cities was something that the Austens would have to cope with. Their Aunt Leigh Perrot's experiences a few years earlier would have alerted the newcomers to the nature of the city which they had recently chosen to be their home.

Bath, like any commercial centre, existed for its customers and not all tradesmen could be trusted to observe purely honest means of finding their profits. Events such as the following, when Mrs Leigh Perrot goes shopping to buy lace, exemplify the caution that the wary exercised amid the bustle of shops and markets.

On 8th August, 1799, Jane's aunt and uncle, sixty and sixty-two years old respectively and a very well respected couple in Bath, set out for a haberdasher's shop in Stall Street, where Mrs Leigh Perrot bought and paid for a length of black lace. On leaving the shop to rejoin her husband Aunt Leigh Perrot was followed and stopped by the shopkeeper who demanded to be allowed to examine the parcel of lace. On being opened it was found to contain some white lace as well as the black that Jane's aunt had purchased. Thinking little of the incident, and seeing it as a simple error, the Leigh

Dixon's View of Bath. Although dating from 1822, this view must have retained much of the Bath Jane Austen knew well. Bath Reference Library.

Price of STOCKS this day at two o'clock.
3 per cent. conf. 63¼. 4 per cent. conf. 79¼. Bank ftock, 168. 3 per cent. red. 61⅜ 5 per cent. Navy, fhut. Long An. 13⅜. Short An. 5⅜. India ftock, fhut. Irifh 5 per cent. 91⅛. Exchequer bills, 4s difc. Omnium, 10¼ pr. Imp. 3 per cent. 59¾. Irifh Lottery Tickets 8l. 8s. 5 per cent. 1797, 95⅞. Englifh Lottery Tickets 15l. 12s.

BATH, Wednesday June 17.

ARRIVED HERE,

Lord Carbery, Lady Boyd, Lady Horton, Sir J. Poore, General Balfour, Col. Brook, Major Plenderleath, Dr. Lind and family, Dr. Evans, Capt. Birchall, Mr. & Mrs. Turner, Mr. and Mifs Hill, Mr. Arden, Mr. J. Balfour, Mr. Alcock, Mr. Maſkelyn, Mr. Graham, Mr. Foſter, Mr. Brander, Mr. Hill, Mr. Baker, Mr. Poore, Mr. Harriſon, Mr. Berry, Mr. Gitton, Mrs. Goddard, Mrs. Morgans, Mrs. Smith, Mrs. Barnwell, Mrs. Auſten, Mrs. Lambert, Mrs. Chapman, Mifs Freeman, Mifs Ferrys, &c. &c.

BATH, May 13th, 1801.

AS MRS. DART's Term for Renting the THREE PUMP-ROOMS

Expires at MIDSUMMER next, fhe refpectfully intreats the Inhabitants and Vifitors, who have drank the Waters at either of them, during that term, will be pleafed to pay her at the BAR of the GREAT PUMP-ROOM; and the Attendants at the refpective Pumps.

Perrots went on their way. A few days later Mrs Leigh Perrot was arrested. The shopkeeper had claimed that she had stolen the white lace and had laid a charge of theft against her. The Mayor and magistrates had no choice but to place Mrs Leigh Perrot under arrest in Ilchester gaol to await trial at the next assizes. Her husband insisted on accompanying her to gaol and so the two old people spent some weeks awaiting trial. Were the outcome to go against Mrs Leigh Perrot, it could have meant transportation to Botany Bay for as long as fourteen years. Despite his gout, Jane's uncle stayed at his wife's side during what must have been a terrible ordeal:

> . . . to prison I was sent – my dearest affectionate husband ill as he was never left me – his tenderness has been beyond description – After about 17 weeks confinement, with his large Shoe, and unable to move without two Sticks, he has never seemed to have a thought but for me.

Mrs Austen offered Jane and Cassandra as companions to their aunt during this sad time, but the old lady resolutely and considerately declined 'to have two

The Bath Chronicle list of visitors for 18th June 1801 which includes Mrs Austen's name. We know that Jane stayed in Bath with her mother in that month.

Sydney Gardens Bath, c.1804. The Austen family lived across the road from these pleasure gardens where they could hear concerts of music and see firework displays. Jane, however, often enjoyed getting as far away from music as possible, being more interested in watching people than in listening to concerts. Victoria Art Gallery, Bath.

Young Creatures gazed at in a public Court' as it 'would cut one to the very heart'.

The trial which took place at Taunton on March 29th 1800 attracted considerable public interest. After nearly six hours of examination the jury returned a verdict of not guilty taking a mere seven and half minutes to reach their decision.

Clearly, as most of the commentators saw it, an attempt had been made to extort money as a bribe to avoid prosecution. The Leigh Perrot's stoicism had prevailed and they kept their good name.

This whole episode serves to remind us of the background against which Jane Austen lived and wrote. In no way was she sheltered from the harshness of a period in English history when the statutory punishment for the theft of a length of lace was hanging or transportation. There would be much relief in the Austen family at the outcome of the trial, but this does not alter the fact that they had been thoroughly involved in the realities of a world in which such things could occur.

4 SYDNEY TERRACE

The Austen family first lived in lodgings, from which they did a considerable amount of house-hunting, finding one house too damp:

> Mr. Philips was very willing to raise the kitchen floor:– but all this I fear is fruitless–tho' the water may be kept out of sight, it cannot be sent away, nor the ill effects of its nearness be excluded, ...
> [Letter to Cassandra, 26 May 1801]

and another too small:

> Yesterday morning we looked at a house in Seymour Street ... but this house was not inviting:– the largest room downstairs was not much more than fourteen feet square, with a western aspect, ...
> [Letter to Cassandra, 12 May 1801]

They finally took out a lease on the house at 4 Sydney Terrace, a house in a row of others, next to the pleasure gardens, from which, as Jane was quick to point out, she could go into the labyrinth every morning. This house seemed to please the family, though Bath gave rise to many quiet complaints:

> In the evening I hope you honoured my Toilette & Ball with a thought; I dressed

myself as well as I could, and had all my finery much admired at home. By nine o'clock my Uncle Aunt & I entered the rooms & linked Miss Winstone on to us.—Before tea, it was rather a dull affair; but then the before tea did not last long, for there was only one dance, danced by four couple.—Think of four couple, surrounded by about a hundred people, dancing in the Upper Rooms at Bath! After tea we *cheered up*; the breaking up of private parties sent some scores more to the Ball, & though it was shockingly and inhumanly thin for this place, there were people enough, I suppose to have made five or six very pretty Basingstoke assemblies.

[Letter to Cassandra, 12 May 1801]

The letters from Sydney Terrace tell a fairly predictable story of life in Bath, with the Austen family engaging in all the usual pastimes. *The Historic and Local New Bath Guide* of 1802 gives a good account of what these might be:

'There are two Dress Balls every week, viz, on Monday at the New Rooms (the Upper Rooms), and on Friday at the Lower Rooms . . . There are also two Fancy Balls every week . . . and nine Subscription Concerts, and three Choral Nights, in the winter at the New Rooms.'

Moreover, Sydney Gardens, where the Austens had their house, was itself one of the most highly developed attractions in Bath, as Pierce Egan in *Walks Through Bath* describes:

'Upon gala nights, the music, singing, cascades, transparencies, fireworks, and superb illuminations, render these gardens very similar to Vauxhall.'

Shopping, card parties, visits to the theatre, taking drives in carriages, all became a normal part of life:

I am just returned from my airing in the very bewitching Phaeton & four, for which I was prepared by a note for Mr. E. soon after breakfast: we went to the top of Kingsdown & had a very pleasant drive: One pleasure succeeds another rapidly.

[Letter to Cassandra, 26 May 1801]

But there were sadnesses and disappointments during the few years that Jane and her family lived at 4 Sydney Terrace. Soon after their arrival her mother, who never enjoyed robust health, if we are to believe Jane's frequent references to her various disorders, became quite seriously ill. With careful nursing she recovered and we have a verse of her own composition to celebrate the recovery:

Says Death 'I've been trying these three weeks and more
To seize an old Madam here at Number Four,
Yet I still try in vain, tho' she turned of three score;

The old theatre in Bath in 1804. Victoria Art Gallery, Bath.

To what is my ill success owing?'
'I'll tell you old Fellow, if you cannot guess,
To what you're indebted for your ill success—
To the prayers of my husband, whose love I possess,
To the care of my daughters, whom Heaven will bless
To the skill and attention of Bowen'

[Bowen was a doctor who practised in Bàth]

The 'old Madam' was to live on for another twenty years.

Mrs Leigh Perrot, Jane's aunt who lived in the Paragon Buildings, Bath. Jane Austen's House, Chawton.

It was during these years that Harris Bigg-Withers made his unexpected proposal to Jane (see Chapter 9) and also that she and her family spent holidays at the seaside, at Sidmouth, Ramsgate and Lyme Regis. With each visit there was to be a romance, either real or fictitious.

At Sidmouth, according to family tradition, Jane fell in love, a love at 'First Impressions', with a young clergyman. Her elder brother James wrote in his *Memoir*:

'Many years after her death, some circumstances induced her sister Cassandra to break through her habitual reticence, and to speak of it. She said that, while staying at some seaside place, they became acquainted with a gentleman, whose charm of person, mind and manners was such that Cassandra thought him worthy to possess and likely to win her sister's love. When they parted, he expressed his intention of soon seeing them again; and Cassandra felt no doubt as to his motives. But they never again met. Within a short time they heard of his sudden death. I believe that, if Jane ever loved, it was this unnamed gentleman; but the acquaintance had been short, and I am unable to say whether her feelings were of such a nature as to affect her happiness.'

This romance remains a mystery, even the separate reports in the family conflict and are at variance. It seems probable, however, that there *was* a young man and that Jane was in love. It is ironic that like her sister Cassandra, Jane should find herself tragically thwarted.

The romance at Ramsgate on the other hand was not Jane's but her brother Frank's, and was with Mary Gibson who was to become a great friend as well as a sister-in-law to Jane and Cassandra.

The romance at Lyme Regis was the fictitious one explored in the novel *Persuasion* which so clearly conveys Jane Austen's own delight in the little seaside town in its pages:

'. . . a very strange stranger it must be, who does not see charms in the immediate environs of Lyme, to make him wish to know it better. The scenes in its neighbourhood, Charmouth, with its high grounds and extensive sweeps of country, and still more its sweet retired bay, backed by dark cliffs, where fragments of low rock among the sands make it the happiest spot for watching the flow of the tide, for sitting in unwearied contemplation;–the

Pages from The trial of Mrs Leigh Perrot. *Mrs Leigh Perrot was tried for the theft of a length of lace, a charge evidently 'planted' on her in an attempt at blackmail. At one stage Jane Austen's mother suggested that Jane might go to prison with her aunt in order to keep her company. The aunt, who was acquitted of the charge, would not hear of 'so sweet a young thing' in the awful confines of the prison.*

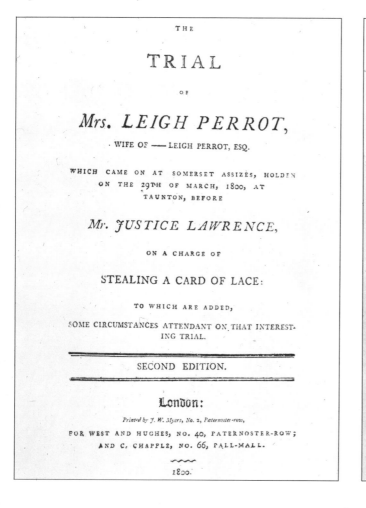

THE

TRIAL

OF

Mrs. LEIGH PERROT,

· WIFE OF —— LEIGH PERROT, ESQ.

WHICH CAME ON AT SOMERSET ASSIZES, HOLDEN ON THE 29TH OF MARCH, 1800, AT TAUNTON, BEFORE

Mr. JUSTICE LAWRENCE,

ON A CHARGE OF

STEALING A CARD OF LACE:

TO WHICH ARE ADDED,

SOME CIRCUMSTANCES ATTENDANT ON THAT INTEREST-ING TRIAL.

SECOND EDITION.

London:

Printed by J. W. Myers, No. 2, Paternoster-row,

FOR WEST AND HUGHES, NO. 40, PATERNOSTER-ROW; AND C, CHAPPLE, NO. 66, PALL-MALL.

1800.

9

brought the note to her for change, which she gave him, and saw him take back to the prisoner.

As soon as witness had given Filby the change, she went down the stairs to dinner, and observed, as she looked round, that the prisoner was moved from the bottom of the counter; but she did not know where to. Prisoner was to pay 1l. 19s. for black lace she had purchased. This was at a time of the year when very little business is done at Bath. There were no goods on the counter on the right hand side of the shop, nor any on the left, excepting the box of black lace, that of white lace, and the veils and handkerchiefs on the brass rod. Miss Rains was down at the desk when witness went to dinner; witness went up again into the shop in about ten minutes afterwards, in consequence of information she had received from Filby; and in about a quarter of an hour after so coming into the shop, she saw the prisoner pass by on the other side of the way with her husband: witness went across to her, and said, " Pray, Madam, have not you a card of white lace as well as of black?" Mrs. Leigh Perrot said, " No,

B

93

woody varieties of the cheerful village of Up Lyme, and, above all, Pinny, with its green chasms between romantic rocks, where the scattered forest trees and orchards of luxuriant growth declare that many a generation must have passed away since the first partial falling of the cliff prepared the ground for such a state, where as scene so wonderful and so lovely is exhibited, as may more than equal any of the resembling scenes of the far-famed Isle of Wight: these places must be visited, and visited again, to make the work of Lyme understood.' [Vol. III, Chapter XI]

We know that Jane Austen bathed at Lyme, following the fashion set by the Prince Regent at Brighton, a fashion that was to detract, in time, from the popularity of Bath:

> The bathing was so delightful this morning &
> Molly so pressing with me to enjoy myself that
> I believe I stayed in rather too long, as since
> the middle of the day I have felt unreasonably
> tired.
> [Letter to Cassandra, 14 September 1804]

Whatever the family comings and goings during the few years at Sydney Place, Jane did not altogether neglect her writing. She tells us herself that the novel which we know as *Northanger Abbey*, at first entitled *Susan*, was *finished* in 1803, in the middle of her time at Bath. It seems likely that she kept writing, particularly

No. 4 Sydney Terrace, Bath. The house where the Austen family lived on Rev George Austen's retirement, and from where Jane chronicled life in Bath.

The Old Ferry, near Bath. Jane Austen revelled in the pleasant country walks around Bath. Victoria Art Gallery, Bath.

as she was to draw upon her own experiences in Bath and elsewhere in other works.

While living in Bath she met with a further set-back to her writing, however; once more with a publisher. In the Spring of 1803, an employee of her brother Henry, a Mr Seymour, wrote to Messrs Crosby and Co., a London publisher, offering them the manuscript novel *Susan*. To everyone's delight the publishers accepted the manuscript and offered a modest payment of £10. It looked as if what had been hoped for was about to happen. Jane Austen had earnt some money, for the first time in her life, and could be confident that her writing was worth publishing. But *Susan* was not published. The book was *advertized* as *Susan: a Novel in Two Volumes*, but never appeared. There is no explanation as to what happened, neither from Jane nor from the publisher. We have to wait six years before we next find any reference to the baffling episode.

After the success of *Sense and Sensibility* in 1809 Jane Austen wrote to Crosby & Co. under the splendid assumed name of 'Mrs Ashton Dennis':

Gentlemen,
In the spring of the year 1803 a MS Novel in 2 vol. entitled Susan was sold to you by a Gentleman of the name of Seymour, & the purchase money £10 rec'd at the same time.

Six years have since passed, & this work of which I am myself the Authoress, has never to the best of my knowledge, appeared in print, tho' an early publication was stipulated for at the time of the sale. I can only account for such an extraordinary circumstance by supposing the MS, by some carelessness to have been lost; and if that was the case, am willing to supply you with another copy if you are disposed to avail yourself of it, & will engage for no further delay when it comes into your hands. It will not be in my power from particular circumstances to command this copy before the Month of August, but then, if you accept my proposal, you may depend on receiving it. Be so good as to send me a line in answer as soon as possible, as my stay in this place will not exceed a few days. Should no notice be taken of this address, I shall feel myself at liberty to secure the publication of my work, by applying elsewhere.

M.A.D.

Direct to Mrs. Ashton Dennis
Post Office Southampton

The letter worked. 'Mrs Ashton Dennis' bought back her manuscript for the amount she had received for it six

Pulteney Street, Bath, in 1820. Bath Reference Library.

years before. One wonders what Crosby & Co. made of their transaction with Mrs Dennis when the manuscript which they had 'held' for so long was published as *Northanger Abbey* by Jane Austen!

But this is to anticipate. Much was to happen before Jane Austen found the confidence that the above letter displays, and before she left Bath.

In January of 1805 Jane's father was taken ill with one of the feverish attacks that had begun to occur soon after the move from Steventon. The illness, 'of only eight and forty hours' carried him off suddenly but peacefully – 'he was spared all the pain of separation, and he went off almost in his sleep' – and Jane was to write to her brother Frank telling him that they had lost 'an Excellent Father'.

The years at Bath were mixed for Jane Austen, and her dismay at the prospect at leaving Steventon seems more poignant when we consider some of the disappointments that she underwent amid the glaring white stone of that elegant city. It is perhaps more pleasing to remember some of the joy that she found in those years of loss and frustration by recalling the walks – along the canal, over Sion Hill and up Beechen Cliff—that gave her such delight, walks that can still be taken today. Her love of the landscape and the countryside reflect the harmony and affection which she knew in her family. The story of Jane Austen in Bath is a story of a close family maintaining its bonds of affection. From the extraordinary tale of Aunt Leigh Perrot's trial to Jane's own description of her father's death we find ourselves listening to a tale of compassion, kindness in adversity and gentle appreciation of consideration. Whatever else befell them in their time out of Hampshire, the Austen family retained their warm supportive unity. Through all the teasing, irony and irritation of the letters of this period, the sense of a loving family shines out. The end of Jane's letter to her brother announcing George Austen's death conveys the poise of the whole family:

My Mother bears the Shock as well as possible; she was quite prepared for it & feels all the blessing of his being spared a long illness. My Uncle and Aunt have been with us, & shew us every imaginable kindness. And tomorrow we shall I dare say have the comfort of James's presence, as an express has been sent to him.– We write also to Godmersham and Brompton. Adieu my dearest Frank. The loss of such a Parent must be felt, or we should be Brutes–. I wish I could have given you better preparation–but it has been impossible.–

Yours Ever affec'ly,
J.A.

[Letter to Frank Austen, 21 January 1805]

Lyme Regis, the setting for Persuasion *and for Jane's own sea-bathing, and a town that she very much enjoyed. The seaside towns rapidly challenged the spas as places of recreation during Jane's lifetime. Her last unfinished novel* Sanditon *is about the development of a seaside resort. Philpot Museum, Lyme Regis.*

Top: Godmersham Park in Kent, from a painting by W. Walter, 1780. The great house that Edward Austen inherited. Here from time to time Jane enjoyed what she called 'life à la Godmersham'. Her brothers hunted in Edward's parkland, played billiards and entertained in a style that amused Jane. Writing from Godmersham in 1813 she commented 'At this present time I have five tables, Eight & twenty chairs & two fires all to myself.' Mr Peter Brooke.

Above: A painting by Malton showing the construction of the Royal Crescent, Bath. Completed in 1774, the design of the Crescent by the second John Wood marked a highly influential advance in town planning. In Jane Austen's time, the Crescent was right at the very edge of Bath, at a place where rough unmetalled roads merged onto paved ones – a feature which made the town such a novelty. Victoria Art Gallery, Bath.

James and Henry

WHEN the Rev George Austen died in 1805, he was buried in the churchyard of Walcot church where he had been married in April 1764. His death meant that the three ladies of the Austen family needed help. The help came from his three older sons, James, Edward and Henry who together produced an income to support the widowed Mrs Austen, and their sisters Jane and Cassandra.

By this time the Austens had moved from 4 Sydney Place and were living at 27 Green Park Buildings where they were to remain until April. Plans were afoot for Martha Lloyd to come to live with them, and these eventually came to fruition with Martha becoming part of the Austen household.

By 1805 three of Jane's brothers were already married and she had a fine number of nephews and nieces. From 1793 with the birth of Anna Austen and Fanny Knight there had been a child almost every year and Jane was well into her famed 'aunthood'. But her brothers were more to her than the providers of nephews, nieces and sisters-in-law. It was through her abiding interest in their careers that she was so well informed about the larger world outside a lady's social circle. By 1805 all her brothers, except the mysterious and unfortunate George, were established with promising careers. One was a wealthy landowner, one a clergyman, two were making their way in the navy and the other in business in London.

From the early days when Jane had watched her brothers from Oxford rehearsing plays in their barn theatre and had seen Frank and Charles set off for the Royal Naval Academy at Portsmouth, her brothers were never far from her thoughts. Her surviving letters carry as much detailed reference to their careers as they do details of hair-styles and dress-patterns.

In a man's world a young lady was fortunate to have brothers, and Jane was especially so to get on so well with hers. In the next two years, her life was more than usually interwoven with theirs and we often find accounts of her setting off in their carriages for visits, or of her staying at their various homes.

The widowed mother and her daughters do not seem to have been able to settle in Bath after George Austen's death. By the summer of 1806 they had left Bath for good. Frank married Mary Gibson, the lady whom Jane had liked so much at Ramsgate, and 1806 found Mrs Austen, her two daughters and Martha Lloyd staying with Frank and Mary in Southampton. By March 1807 the ladies had moved into a house in Castle Square

A satirical view of an eighteenth-century country vicar. British Museum, London.

which had the great advantage of its own garden and was where they lived until their return to Hampshire in 1809. Although there is little evidence of Jane doing any writing while in Southampton, her letters to Cassandra dating from those days show her to have been happy. The arrangements for their house and garden seem to have kept her both happy and busy:

> Our Garden is putting in order, by a Man who bears a remarkably good character . . . at my own particular desire he procures for us some Syringas. I could not do without a Syringa for the sake of Cowper's Line . . .
>
> . . . Our Dressing-Table is constructing on the spot, out of a large Kitchen Table belonging to the House, for doing which we have the permission of Mr. Husket Lord Lansdown's Painter,– domestic painter I should call him, for he lives in the Castle. Domestic Chaplains have given way to this more necessary Office, and I suppose whenever the walls want no touching up, he is employed about my Lady's face.
>
> [Letter to Cassandra, 8 February 1807]

Later in the same letter Jane teases Cassandra on her new sister-in-law's behalf:

For about three years Jane, Cassandra and their mother lived in Southampton, in Castle Square near to the fairy-land castle that the Marquis of Landsdowne had built. The Marchioness would drive from the castle in 'a light phaeton, drawn by six and sometimes eight little ponies, each pair decreasing in size and becoming lighter in colour, . . . as it was placed farther away from the carriage'. (J. E. Austen Leigh, Memoir.)

> Frank & Mary cannot at all approve of your not being at home in time to help them in their finishing purchases [Cassandra was staying with her brother Edward at Godmersham Park in Kent], & desire me to say that, if you are not, they shall be as spiteful as possible & chuse everything in the stile most likely to vex you, knives that will not cut, glasses that will not hold, a sofa without a seat, & a Bookcase without shelves.
>
> [Ibid]

It says much for the new Mrs Austen that she can so readily be included in the gentle teasing that the family seem always to have enjoyed. The generous acceptance of Mary Gibson is typical of the Austen family. Time and time again the tone of their letters and the spirit of

Above: An illustration done by Hugh Thompson in 1890 of a scene from Persuasion: *'A gentleman politely drew back.' Jane Austen's House, Chawton.*

Opposite top: A Rowlandson cartoon from The Comforts of Bath. *The 'gouty' husband plods behind the fashionable beau who captures the young wife's attention. The world of Bath 'society' is cleverly captured by an accomplished draughtsman.*

Opposite bottom: The Pump Room, Bath, *by J. C. Nattes. Queen Anne's visits to Bath in 1702 and 1703 made the town, which was already renowned for the medical qualities of its waters, a fashionable resort. It is a fine example of a town which was developed as a pleasure resort. The pump room was as much a social meeting place as a medical centre. Victoria Art Gallery, Bath.*

St John's College, Oxford, in a cartoon by
Rowlandson. This was the college where Jane's father
and her two brothers were educated. The Library, St
John's College, Oxford.

their endeavour is to include, to share and embrace
others with the same affection that they appear to have
for each other. Any study of any single member of that
family is at once a glimpse of a group of people whose
fortunes overlap and whose concerns seem always to be
for each other. From the Rev George Austen and his
wife there must have flowed a degree of consideration
and tolerance that bred harmony. It is this harmony,
more than any other feature, that shines through all of
Jane's surviving letters.

The various careers of Jane's brothers provide a
commentary upon eighteenth-century life. Through
them she could be conversant with many current and
significant events.

Jane's eldest brother, the Rev James Austen, must not
be overlooked in any consideration of her brothers'
influence upon her life and attitudes. Although a
clergyman, he was no simple continuance of his father,
The fact that he took over the parish of Steventon on his
father's retirement in 1801 does not mean that his
ministry was the same, or his theology identical with

that of his celebrated scholar father. James was his own
man and perhaps the confidence with which he pulled
down the old rectory and had a new one built suggests
the measure of his independence.

It has become commonplace to undervalue the
importance of religion in Jane Austen's writing. Together with Charlotte Brontë she is remembered as a
severe critic of curates and, apparently, of the teachings
of Christianity. Such an erroneous estimate of the value
both women placed upon the 'Christian' way of life is
unfortunate and misleading. Because a writer shows a
bad example, because Jane Austen gives us the Mr
Eltons of this world, we must not be deaf to her more
sober statements about the importance of religion, and
of the central tenets of Christianity, that inform her
whole moral vision. The scene in the chapel of *Mansfield
Park* is of greater significance than has usually been
realized. Jane Austen's description of the chapel and of
the events that take place in it in this scene would be
inconceivable to her father's generation, and belongs
wholly to the time of her brother's ministry, embodying
its preoccupations rather than those of the previous
generation:

'They entered. Fanny's imagination had prepared her
for something grander than a mere spacious, oblong
room, fitted up for the purpose of devotion – with

nothing more striking or more solemn than the profusion of mahogany, and the crimson velvet cushions appearing over the ledge of the family gallery above. "I am disappointed," said she, in a low voice, to Edmund. "This is not my idea of a chapel. There is nothing awful here, nothing melancholy, nothing grand. Here are no aisles, no arches, no inscriptions, no banners. No banners, cousin, to be 'blown by the night wind of heaven.' No signs that a 'Scottish monarch sleeps below.' "

"You forget, Fanny, how lately all this has been built, and for how confined a purpose, compared with the old chapels of castles and monasteries. It was only for the private use of the family. They have been buried, I suppose, in the parish church. *There* you must look for the banners and the achievements."

"It was foolish of me not to think of all that; but I am disappointed."

Mrs. Rushworth began her relation. "This chapel was fitted up as you see it, in James the Second's time. Before that period, as I understand, the pews were only wainscot; and there is some reason to think that the linings and the cushions of the pulpit and the family-seat were only purple cloth; but this is not quite certain. It is a handsome chapel, and was formerly in constant use

Henry Austen, a scholar, an officer in the Oxford Militia, a bankrupt and eventually a clergyman. It was Henry who helped Jane have her novels published, and he who cheerfully betrayed her secret authorship to friends and acquaintances. Jane Austen's House, Chawton.

James Austen, Jane's eldest brother, a scholar, clergyman and himself a writer. James succeeded to the living of St Nicholas Steventon when his father retired to Bath. Mrs R. M. Lefroy.

both morning and evening. Prayers were always read in it by the domestic chaplain, within the memory of many; but the late Mr. Rushworth left it off."

"Every generation has its improvements," said Miss Crawford, with a smile, to Edmund.' [Vol. I, Chapter IX]

Like so many of Jane Austen's scenes, the episode in the chapel is dense with significance. The old order has passed, and the details of Fanny's romantic expectations, Mrs Rushworth's pat tourist's guide description, Miss Crawford's cutting, but nevertheless fashionable comment, all build up the ironic intention behind the simple account in the story. If we listen carefully we can hear Jane Austen's own voice, a voice quite distinct and separate from those of the characters of her creating. We are left in no doubt as to her view of the way that the world has 'improved' itself by the abandoning of prayer. Miss Crawford continues to pour scorn on the idea of family prayers, suggesting that those who attended in the past only did so under compulsion: '". . . starched up into seeming piety, but with heads full of something very different—especially if the poor chaplain were not worth looking at—and, in those days, I fancy parsons were very inferior even to what they are now."' [Ibid]

Cassandra Austen's watercolour of Fanny Knight,
eldest daughter of Jane Austen's brother Edward. She
was possibly Jane Austen's favourite niece.
'My dearest Fanny,
You are inimitable, irresistible. You are the delight of
my life. Such letters, such entertaining Letters as you
have lately sent! Such a description of your queer little
heart! Such a lovely display of what Imagination does.
You are worth your weight in Gold, or even in the new
silver coinage.'
(Letter to Fanny Knight, 20 February 1817.) Jane
Austen's House, Chawton.

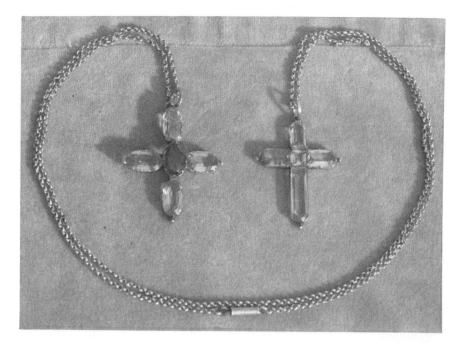

Top: The topaz crosses which Charles Austen, one of Jane's sailor brothers, gave to his sister in 1801: 'He [Charles] has received 30£ for his share of the privateer & expects 10£ more – but of what avail is it to take prizes if he lays out the produce in presents to his sisters. He has been buying gold chains & Topaze crosses for us; – he must be well scolded.' (Letter to Cassandra, 26 May 1801.) Jane Austen's House, Chawton.

Above: Chawton House and Church, in an oil painting dated 1809. Jane's brother Edward owned the house and park, called in those days 'The Great House', but he seldom lived there himself much to his sister's annoyance. Jane's mother and sister are both buried in the churchyard within the park. Jane Austen's House, Chawton.

Miss Crawford is offensive and the rest of the party 'inspecting' the chapel no less so. Julia Bertram who represents the 'new' approach to religion makes irreverent fun of the marriage service (a sacrament), by making a joke of the fact that Mr Rushworth and Maria were standing side by side. She thought that it would be hugely amusing for them to be married there and then: 'nothing in the world could be more snug and pleasant'. ' "If Edmund were but in orders!" cried Julia, and running to where he stood with Miss Crawford and Fanny: "My dear Edmund, if you were but in orders now, you might perform the ceremony." ' [Ibid]

Edmund is in fact intending to take orders, the 'joke' is in bad taste. At the close of the scene which has contained a parody of one of the most important sacraments of the Christian Church, Jane Austen makes her own comment:

'The chapel was soon afterwards left to the silence which reigned in it with few interruptions throughout the year. Miss Bertram, displeased with her sister, led the way, and all seemed to feel that they had been there long enough.' [Ibid]

The image of an abandoned chapel with the implication that it represented a neglect of all that its use should imply, is a powerful one. It is not too much to imagine that the house that can so abuse its chapel and ignore the peace it offers might be called a 'godless' one. The jesting about marriage is quite out of place. It is perhaps worth remembering that Jane Austen wrote prayers as well as novels. The inscription on her grave in Winchester Cathedral records her faith and not her success as a writer of fiction.

Later in *Mansfield Park* Edmund discusses his vocation with Miss Crawford and he is quite explicit about the duties of a clergyman. He refutes the idea that being a good preacher is all that is required and puts a case which might well have been argued for Jane's father or her two brothers in the Church.

It is probably impossible to over-estimate the effect that the country parsonage childhood had upon Jane's values and attitude to life. Her reading, her scholar father and her brothers do not appear to have been narrow sombre influences; on the contrary their brand of religion seems to have been one of joy and sympathy. Edmund Bertram's defence of the country clergy may offer us some clues about the three clergymen that Jane knew best, the Rev George, the Rev James and the Rev Henry Austen:

' "We do not look in cities for our best morality. It is not there that respectable people of any denomination can do most good; and it certainly is not there that the influence of the clergy can be most felt. A fine preacher is followed and admired; but it is not in fine preaching only that a good clergyman will be useful in his parish and his neighbourhood, where the parish and neighbourhood are of a size capable of knowing his private character, and observing his general conduct, which in London can rarely be the case. The clergy are lost there in the crowds of their parishioners. They are known to the largest part only as preachers. And with regard to their influencing public matters, Miss Crawford must not misunderstand me, or suppose I mean to call them the arbiters of good breeding, the regulators of refinement and courtesy, the masters of the ceremonies of life. The *manners* I speak of might rather be called *conduct*, perhaps the result of good principles; the effect, in short, of those doctrines which it is their duty to teach and recommend; and it will, I believe, be everywhere found, that as the clergy are, or are not what they ought to be, so are the rest of the nation." ' [Ibid]

Henry Austen's influence upon his sister Jane went far beyond the implications of his eventual ordination. Henry's was a chequered career. From university he joined the Oxford Militia rising to the rank of Captain and becoming an Adjutant. This was no sheltered life. He would be involved in the management of men commonly seen as the scum of the earth amongst fellow officers who were susceptible to bribes and corrupt practices. Life in the Militia could be very hard and Henry would know it for what it was. Jane Austen's ballroom lieutenants would have real life, and less romantic counterparts in Henry's fellow militiamen.

From the Militia, Henry turned to banking: in London with *Austen, Maunde and Tilson*, and in Alton with *Austen, Gray and Vincent*. But his banking career ended in disaster. After rising to become Receiver General for Oxfordshire in 1813 he became a bankrupt in 1816. It was after this that he was ordained.

Henry was a favourite of Jane Austen's. After the Comte de la Feuillide had been executed in France, his widow, Eliza, had virtually 'pursued' the then unmarried Austen brothers. Much against his mother's advice Henry married his cousin Eliza in 1797. It was with Eliza and Henry that Jane Austen stayed when visiting London. And it was with Henry's encouragement and help that her books came to be published.

Edward, Frank and Charles

'Yesterday passed quite à la Godmersham'

LIFE 'à la Godmersham' was only possible because Jane's older brother Edward had been adopted by the Knight family and had thereby inherited large estates. It was through Edward's good fortune, and to be just, through his proven ability to manage the estates that he inherited that the Austen family lived in the comfort that they did. Godmersham Park in Kent, the home of the Knight family, passed to Edward who, in the year 1812, changed his name finally from Austen to Knight. From time to time Jane and Cassandra stayed at the house – Cassandra being a more frequent visitor than Jane – where they were able to taste some of the advantages of living in fine style.

Jane never seems to have fully accepted the 'grandness' of life in a great house although she obviously thoroughly enjoyed the experience.

Mrs Knight, on the death of her husband, made over Godmersham Park to Edward in 1798 and from that date we have records of visits being made by members of the Austen family. From the details of Jane's visits we can see just how far this introduction into a higher class than her own background was to affect Jane Austen, or to provide her with an insight into a higher social circle.

Jane's letters from Godmersham are remarkably balanced. She allows herself to be quietly amused to find herself in the great house, her brother having gone out into his woods:

> . . . all alone. – At this present time I have five Tables, Eight and twenty Chairs & two fires all to myself.
> [Letter to Cassandra, 3 November 1813]

Again and again she records, albeit modestly, the advantages of Edward's way of life:

> Yesterday passed quite à la Godmersham: the gentlemen rode about Edward's farm, and returned in time to saunter along Bentigh with us; and after dinner we visited the Temple

The Royal Naval Academy, Portsmouth, which existed to provide trained officers for a navy with corrupt promotion methods. Two of Jane's brothers were educated here. Portsmouth City Museum and Art Gallery.

Plantations, which to be sure, is a Chevalier Bayard of a Plantation. James and Mary are much struck with the beauty of the place. Today the spirit of the thing is kept up by the two brothers being gone to Canterbury in the chair.
> [Letter to Cassandra, 15 June 1808]

We must not mistake. Jane Austen may have written only of what she knew well, but at Godmersham Park she saw more than village life and, while retaining her sense of perspective, knew what it was to live in luxury:

> Bread has sunk & is likely to sink more, which we hope may make Meat sink too. But I have no occasion to think of the price of Bread, or of Meat where I am now; – let me shake off vulgar cares & conform to the happy Indifference of East Kent wealth.
> [Letter to Frank Austen, 25 September 1813]

In this same letter she describes a meeting of the family which gives the lie to the notion that she lived obscurely and frugally, being solely concerned with her writing:

> We left Chawton on ye 14th, – spent two entire days in Town & arrived here on ye 17th, – My Br, Fanny, Lizzy, Marrianne & I composed this division of the Family, and filled his Carriage, inside and out. – Two post-chaises under the escort of George conveyed eight more across the Country, the Chair brought two, two others came on horseback & the rest by the Coach – & so by one means or another we are all removed. – It puts me in mind of the account of St. Paul's shipwreck, when all are

Jany 27. -1817.

A Gentleman & Lady travelling from Tun-
bridge towards that part of the Sussex
Coast which lies between Hastings &
E. Bourne, being induced by Business to quit
the high road, & attempt a very rough Lane,
were overturned in toiling up
its long ascent — half rock, half sand. — The accident
happened just beyond the only Gentleman's
House near the Lane — the House, which
their Driver on being required to take that
direction, had intimated to be necessarily their
object, & had with most unwilling Looks
been constrained to pass by — He had
grumbled & shaken his shoulders so much
indeed, & seemed so delighting in his Horses so
sharply, that he might have been open to
the suspicion of overturning them on purpose:
(especially as the Carriage was not his Master's
own) if the road had not indisputably become
considerably worse than before, as soon as the
premises of the said House were left behind —
most intelligent & attentive
countenance, that beyond it no wheels but Cart
wheels could safely proceed.

that Loveliness was
complete.

Above: Hanover Square, London, in a coloured engraving by R. Pollard and F. Jukes after E. Dayes, dated 1787. Coloured engravings were very popular in the eighteenth century. The scene shown here is typical of the fashionable parts of London that Jane Austen knew well from her visits to her brother Henry. The high-sprung curricle, surely exaggerated here, suggests the precarious nature of this fashionable means of transport and the risk that the 'high fliers' who rode in them took.

Opposite top: The showroom of Wedgwood & Byerley in London, a showroom which Jane Austen visited in search of table-ware: 'We then went to Wedgwoods where my brother and Fanny chose a Dinner Set. I believe the pattern is a small-Lozenge in purple, between Lines of narrow Gold; – & it is to have the crest.' (Letter to Cassandra, 23 September 1813.) The dinner service is to be seen at Jane Austen's Chawton home.

Opposite bottom: The first page of the manuscript of the novel upon which Jane Austen was working during her final illness. The incomplete manuscript, now commonly known as Sanditon, *is the only document of Jane Austen's maturity to have survived which gives us some idea of her writing methods. The last sentence was written on 18th March 1817: in July of the same year Jane Austen was dead. King's College Library, Cambridge.*

An illustration that demonstrates the kind of 'improvement' recommended by Mr Repton. The art of landscaping, the art of 'the picturesque', interested Jane Austen. In Mansfield Park and Northanger Abbey she makes use of her knowledge of this late-eighteenth-century enthusiasm. The illustrations show the 'before and after' improvement. It was Lancelot Brown's ability to find grounds 'capable' of improvement that earnt him the nickname 'Capability Brown'. Jane Austen found the preoccupation with the picturesque mildly amusing, and a source of comedy in her novels.

said by different means to reach the shore in safety.

[Letter to Frank Austen, 25 September 1813]

Carriages, chairs, post-chaises, the list is almost as long as those that Jane Austen used to humorous effect in her early parodies. While staying with Edward, Jane would experience and witness much that sums up the life of the leisured class in late eighteenth- and early nineteenth-century rural England:

> Now these two Boys who are out with the Foxhounds will come home & disgust me again by some habit of Luxury, or some proof of sporting mania – unless I keep it off by this prediction.
>
> [Letter to Cassandra, 11 October 1813]

We hear of the 'comfort of the Billiard Table', how it draws all the gentlemen to it whenever they are indoors, conveniently leaving the ladies the library to themselves. There are frequent references to shooting parties, to race meetings and, above all, to the number and rank of visitors:

> Yesterday was a day of dissipation all through, first came Sir Brook [Edward's father-in-law, Sir Brook Bridges] to dissipate us before breakfast – then there was a call from Mr. Sherer, then a regular morning visit from Lady Honeywood . . .
>
> [Letter to Cassandra, 6 November 1813]

It was on this visit that Jane confessed to a hidden advantage to be gained from growing older (she was now almost thirty-eight):

> By the bye, as I must leave off being young, I find many Douceurs in being a sort of Chaperon for I am put on the Sofa near the Fire & can drink as much wine as I like.
>
> [Ibid]

One of the joys of her stays at Godmersham was the company of her young nephews and nieces, and we shall see further on how much this meant to the lady who took such a pride in 'good Auntship'. Edward and Elizabeth had eleven children in all, five girls and six boys. All were to know their Aunt Jane well.

Edward Austen's translation into Edward Knight materially altered the course of Jane Austen's life. Not only did it bring her into contact with nobility and life among the leisured class, but it eventually provided her with a roof over her head in the village of Chawton, of which the Manor House was another of Edward's houses. At the time that Edward changed his name to Knight, Jane's typically wry comment was merely that she must 'learn to make a better 'K' '.

Edward Austen was eventually to become a wealthy and successful landowner, and it is interesting to reflect upon his involvement with the harsh laws governing poaching in this capacity. Whatever it was that made

Edward Austen (later Knight), Jane's elder brother who was adopted by a wealthy relative, Thomas Knight of Godmersham in Kent. Edward was to become a rich landowner. Major Edward Knight, Chawton House.

Jane Austen leave such matters out of her novels, or if they were included to keep them at the periphery, it was by no means ignorance or naivety. Edward would know the game laws and it seems likely that Jane Austen would too.

FRANK AND CHARLES

Frank and Charles Austen are the most colourful of Jane's brothers, and possibly the most surprising: they were both admirals. Both left home while quite young to attend the Royal Naval Academy at Portsmouth and both served for many years in a navy that saw action in almost every corner of the globe.

Francis, known to Jane as Frank, was fourteen when he went to Portsmouth and Charles, whom Jane called 'our own particular little brother', for he was the only child of the family younger than herself, was only twelve. But by the standards of the day they could almost be considered veterans: young boys of only *nine* years were to be found entrusted to the 'tender' care of captains. One such boy wrote home to his father saying that the captain had allowed him to sleep in his own cabin and, because he was so young, had not yet made him climb higher than the first yard-arm. But such consideration was unusual. The historian Halevy, writing in *England in 1815*, leaves us in no doubt about the Navy:

'The English fleets about the year 1800 still represented the old England of the eighteenth century, riotous and insubordinate. The ships that won the day at Camper-

Above: A page from a book of songs copied out in Jane Austen's hand, showing the kind of song that would be sung in the drawing rooms of her novels. Jane Austen's House, Chawton.

Top: A patchwork quilt, worked by Jane and her mother. Jane was considered to be a dextrous needlewoman, and all the surviving examples of her work bear witness to her neatness and skill. Mrs Christopher Knight.

A Man-Trap. Throughout Jane's life harsh game laws were in force protecting the property of the rich against the necessity of the poor: game was preserved in areas where food was scarce, and man-traps and spring-guns inflicting hideous wounds were legal in private grounds.

down, Cape St. Vincent, and Aboukir were commanded by undisciplined officers, and manned by mutinous crews.'

We cannot argue a special case for Jane's brothers. They were in the navy during the most serious and total mutinies that the Royal Navy was ever to experience, and, what is more, they both proved successful within whatever kind of corrupt organization the fleet that guarded England might have been.

Discipline in the navy was harsh and its recruiting methods appalling. As officers Frank and Charles would be involved in both maintaining good order and keeping together crews. Men could be 'pressed' into service, which really amounted to being kidnapped, and made to serve in dreadful conditions where punishments were extreme. A ballad of the day suggests the plight of those unfortunate enough to live by ports:

> The Voyage was past and England's shore,
>   Had met my longing View,
> I left the Ship and sought the COT?
>   That held my lovely SUE!
> She flew to meet me in each eye,
>   The tear of Joy had started,
> Thank Heaven thou art safe my love:
>   She cry'd, we'll never more be parted.
>
> The lovely BOYS my Susan brought,
>   They hung about my knees,
> Now let who will be Kings he said,
>   Give me such joys as these;
> Just as I spoke a press-gang came,
>   Poor GIRL she shrieked and started,
> She caught my hand and cried dear JACK
>   I fear we must be parted.
>
> My Children wept, in vain I told;
>   How long I'd been away,
> They said the King required my aid,
>   They dare not disobey,
> My Susan cried it's hard my love
>   But be thou not faint-hearted,
> The powers above will reward my love,
>   Then sobbed adieu and parted.

[A broadsheet quoted in *Adventures of a Naval Officer 1801–1812* by Admiral Jackson]

Captain Charles Austen, Jane's younger brother. Jane Austen's House, Chawton.

Admiral Sir Francis Austen. Jane Austen's House, Chawton.

*Above: A satirical cartoon of Portsmouth which
conveys something of the flavour of life in Nelson's
navy, the navy of Jane's brothers Frank and Charles.*

Below: The midshipmen's berth.

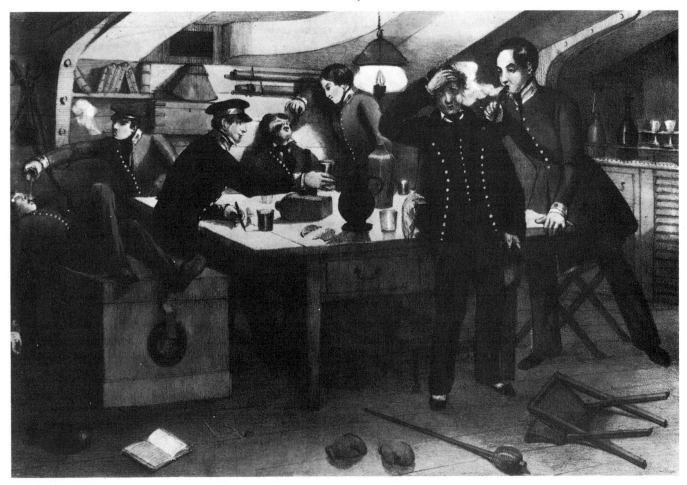

Rowlandson's drawing of the uniform of a midshipman in 1799: the uniform that Jane's brothers might have worn.

Perhaps when we read that Richard Parker, who had been one of the instigators of the 1797 mutiny which affected every fleet in the navy, was tried and executed on board the *Neptune*, a ship to which Frank Austen was appointed Flag Captain in 1801, we can see how close Jane Austen was to some of the less elegant activities of her world.

Frank Austen was to end up with a knighthood, the Order of the Bath (a much coveted distinction, as there were only a small number of knights with that order),

HMS Vindictive. *The flagship of Vice-Admiral Sir Francis Austen, Jane's brother Frank, with whom she lived for a while in Southampton. Jane Austen's House, Chawton.*

while Charles ended his career as Commander in Chief on the North American and West Indies station.

Jane Austen's references to sailors, to the Navy and to life aboard ship derive from her brothers' experience. As we might expect, the references in her novels are accurate and informed, often relating quite specifically to events in her brothers' careers. She even names her brothers' ships in her stories, after seeking their permission:

> I have something in hand which I hope on the credit of P. & P. will sell well . . . And by the bye—shall you object to my mentioning the Elephant in it, and two or three other of your old Ships. I *have* done it, but it shall not stay to make you angry. They are only just mentioned.
>
> [Letter to Frank Austen, 3 July 1813]

The 'something in hand' was *Mansfield Park*.

Charles Austen married while away from home, his bride Frances Palmer being the daughter of the Attorney General for Bermuda. When he did return to England it was to bring with him his daughter Cassandra, whose childhood highlights Jane Austen's involvement in the problems that faced naval families. Little Cassandra lived on board ship, on the *Namur*, with her parents. Letters from Jane at Godmersham in 1813 show that there was some concern about her health. She had been sickly and the stay in Kent seemed to have been doing her good:

> Cassy had recovered her looks almost entirely, and I find they do not consider the 'Namur' as disagreeing with her in general, only when the weather is so rough as to make her sick.
>
> [Letter to Cassandra, 26 October 1813]

Her parents were uncertain as to what to do for the best. Jane and her sister Cassandra were all for the little girl staying with them in their house at Chawton—they eventually won—whereas the parents were not at all sure what to do:

> Papa and Mama have not yet made up their mind as to parting with her or not—The chief, indeed the only difficulty with Mama is a very reasonable one, the child's being very unwilling to leave them. When it was mentioned to her, she did not like the idea of it at all: At the same time, she has been suffering so much lately from Sea sickness, that her Mama cannot bear to have her on board this winter.—Charles is less inclined to part with her.
>
> [Letter to Cassandra, 14 October 1813]

Such a discussion lends some weight to the comments in *Persuasion* about whether women should or should not be allowed on board ships. Here, Admiral Croft is speaking:

' "... I hate to hear of women on board, or to see them on board; and no ship under my command shall ever convey a family of ladies any where, if I can help it."

This brought his sister upon him.

"Oh! Frederick! But I cannot believe it of you. All idle refinement! Women may be as comfortable on board as in the best house in England. I believe I have lived as much on board as most women, and I know nothing superior to the· accommodation of a man of war. I declare I have not a comfort or an indulgence about me, even at Kellynch-hall ... beyond what I always had in most of the ships I have lived in; and they have been five altogether." ' [Vol. III, Chapter VIII]

Later she is able to make a fine distinction:

' "... nothing can exceed the accommodations of a man of war, I speak you know of the higher rates. When you come to a frigate, of course, you are more confined..." ' [Ibid]

Jane Austen is on sure ground here as far as her facts are concerned, and the satire is of her best. Charles was on board the *Unicorn* when it engaged and captured *La Tribune*. One of Nelson's sailors at Trafalgar gives the lie to the lady's optimism about life at sea:

Honoured Father,

This comes to tell you I am alive and hearty except three fingers; but that's not much, it might have been my head. I told brother Tom I should like to see a great battle, and I have seen one, and we have peppered the Combined rarely [off Trafalgar]; ... Three of our mess are killed, and four more of us winged. But to tell you the truth of it, when the game began, I wished myself at Warnborough with my plough again; but when they had given us one duster, and I found myself snug and tight, I set to in good earnest, and thought no more about being killed than if I were at Murrell Green Fair, and I was presently as busy and black as a collier. How my fingers got knocked overboard I don't know, but off they are, and I never missed them till I wanted them. You see by my writing it was my left hand.

[A letter from the Lower Deck, 1805]

The above example is a very mild description of what might befall a sailor in a sea battle, but it will serve to remind us of the navy in which Francis and Charles Austen made their way, and to suggest why it might have been advisable for little Cassandra to live with her aunts on dry land.

Jane Austen took more than a passing interest in her brothers' careers. She followed their chances of promotion as keenly as she questioned Cassandra about a new bonnet, or Edward about a new breed of sheep. A letter to Cassandra as early as 1798 shows the interest at home of the sailor brothers' fortunes:

I have got some pleasant news for you ... Admiral Gambier, in reply to my father's application, writes as follows:– 'As it is usual to keep young officers in small vessels it being most proper on account of their inexperience, and it being also a situation where they are more in the way of learning their duty, your son has been continued in the *Scorpion;* but I have mentioned to the Board of Admiralty his wish to be in a frigate, and when a proper opportunity offers and it is judged he has taken his turn in a small ship, I hope he will be removed. With regard to your son in the *London* I am glad I can give you the assurance that his promotion is likely to take place very soon, as Lord Spencer has been so good as to say he would include him in an arrangement that he proposes making in a short time relative to some promotions in that quarter.'

[Letter to Cassandra, 24 December 1798]

The Austen family was a closely knit one. Across the sea as across the counties of England the letters went to and fro. Through her brothers Jane Austen was very well informed of the state of the world beyond her own immediate circle. News was always eagerly sought and awaited wherever she was living. The correspondence continued throughout her life however near or far any relative might be. It is through the remains of that correspondence that we can know so much of the family who lived so long ago. Beyond the biographical details, however, we may also discern some of the experiences and insights that contributed to the development of Jane Austen's literary and artistic skill as well as to her own personal family history.

Nephews and Nieces

'Itty Dordy': 'All the comforts of Little Children — dirt and litter'

JANE AUSTEN set great store by what she called good 'Auntship'. This was not a sentimental indulgence on her part, but more a robust, humorous and loving concern for her nephews and nieces that was in every case reciprocal, and, from the testimony of the nephews and nieces themselves, very much valued.

Her assumptions about children derived from a clear view of what they were and a strong respect for them as individuals with a right, within reason, to their own point of view. She was no romantic about children, but was a shrewd observer of their behaviour. In the opening chapters of *Persuasion*, for example, Anne Elliot is sitting with an invalid boy, when his brother appears on the scene:

Fireplace in the hall of Chawton Manor, one of Edward Knight's houses.

'The younger boy, a remarkable stout, forward child, of two years old, having got the door opened for him by someone without, made his determined appearance among them, and went straight to the sofa to see what was going on, and put in his claim to anything good that might be giving away.

There being nothing to eat, he could only have some play; and as his aunt would not let him tease his sick brother, he began to fasten himself upon her, as she knelt, in such a way that, busy as she was about Charles, she could not shake him off. She spoke to him, ordered, entreated, and insisted in vain. Once she did contrive to push him away, but the boy had the greater pleasure in getting upon her back again directly.' [Vol. III, Chapter IX]

Jane Austen knew children well. In her letters as well as her fiction she understands the advantages of having them in the house:

> One long morning visit is what generally
> occurs, & such a one took place yesterday. We
> went to Baughurst . . . The house seemed to
> have all the comforts of little Children, dirt
> and litter. Mr. Dyson as usual looked wild, &
> Mrs. Dyson as usual looked big.
> [Letter to Cassandra, 11 February 1801]

In her dealings with children she seems to have relied upon her sense of the comic, her extraordinary patience and delight in the unexpected (a disarming combination in an adult):

> My sweet little George! I am delighted to hear
> that he has such an inventive genius as to face-
> making . . . I wore my green shoes last night,
> and took my *white fan* with me; I am very glad
> he never threw it into the river.
> [Letter to Cassandra, 8 January 1799]

George, her brother Edward's third child, was then four years old. A year later Jane mentions him again:

Pray give my love to George, tell him I am very glad to hear he can skip so well already, & that I hope he will continue to send me word of his improvement in the art.

[Letter to Cassandra, 8 January 1801]

Since 1798, when George was three, he had been in the habit of sending his aunt messages. 'Itty Dordy', as he was called from his own first attempts at pronouncing his name, was one of the first nephews in whom Jane could take an interest:

> My dear itty Dordy's remembrance of me is very pleasing to me—foolishly pleasing, because I know it will be over so soon. My attachment to him will be more durable. I shall think with tenderness and delight in his beautiful and smiling countenance and interesting manners till a few years have turned him into an ungovernable, ungracious fellow.
>
> [Letter to Cassandra, 27 October 1798]

In 1814, Cassandra, brother Charles's first daughter, was living with Jane and her sister Cassandra at Chawton. Letters of that period continue the amusement, or loving game that Jane had set in motion. Being herself away from home, Jane sends a message to 'little Cassy' who was then six years old:

> Give my love to little Cassandra! I hope she found my bed comfortable last night and has not filled it with fleas.
>
> [Letter to Cassandra, 2 March 1814]

This 'hope' brought a reply, for a later letter from Jane retorts:

> If Cassandra has filled my Bed with fleas, I am sure they must bite herself.–
>
> [Letter to Cassandra, 9 March 1814]

It appears that the children were included in the letters that Jane and Cassandra wrote to each other. Included, moreover, in more ways than one. Edward, Jane's brother Edward's second child, supplies a good example. He provides this addition to a letter from his aunt to Cassandra:

> My dearest Aunt Cass:
> I have just asked At. Jane to let me write a little in her letter, but she does not like it so I wont.– Goodbye.
>
> [In a letter to Cassandra, 11 October 1813]

Other letters carry other, just as cheerful, messages:

> Fanny desires her love to you [Edward Austen's eldest child, then six years old] her love to grandpapa, her love to Anna, and her

---

The poem that Jane wrote which announces her delight at the prospect of living in the house at Chawton which Edward gave to Jane's mother rent free. Jane Austen's House, Chawton.

Copy of a letter to Frank. July 26. 1809.

My dearest Frank, I wish you joy
Of Mary's safety with a boy,
Whose birth has given little pain,
Compared with that of Mary Jane.
May he a growing Blessing prove,
And well deserve his Parents' Love!
Endow'd with Art's & Nature's Good,
Thy name-possessing with thy Blood;
In him, in all his ways, may we
Another Francis William see!—
Thy infant days may he inherit,
Thy warmth, nay insolence of spirit;
We would not with one fault dispense
To weaken the resemblance.
May he revive thy Nursery sin,
Peeping as daringly within,
(His curley Locks but just descried)
With "Bet my be not come to bide."
Fearless of danger, braving pain,
And threaten'd very oft in vain,
Still may one Terror daunt his soul.
One needful engine of controul
Be found in this sublime array,
A neighbouring Donkey's awful Bray.
So may his equal faults as Child
Produce Maturity as mild.
His saucy words & fiery ways
In early Childhood's pretty days.
In Manhood shew his Father's mind,
Like him considerate & kind;
All Gentleness to those around,
And eager only not to wound.
Then like his Father too, he must,
To his own former struggles, just,
Feel his Deserts with honest glow,
And all his Self-improvement know.
A native fault may thus give birth
To the best blessing, conscious worth.

As for ourselves, we're very well;
As unaffected prose will tell.
Cassandra's pen will give our state
The many comforts that await
Our Chawton home — how much we find
Already in it to our mind,
And how convinced that when complete,
It will all other Houses beat
That ever have been made or mended,
With rooms concise, or rooms distended.

You'll find us very snug next year,
Perhaps with Charles & Fanny near —
For now it often does delight us
To fancy them just over-right us.

J. A.

The concern shown by the nouveaux riches *with the 'accomplishments' of their expensively educated offspring contrasts with Jane Austen's genuine sensitivity to the real needs of children. British Museum, London.*

love to Hannah; the latter is particularly to be remembered. Edward desires his love to you, to grandpapa, to Anna, to little Edward, to Aunt James and Uncle James, and he hopes all your turkeys and ducks, and chicken and guinea fowls are very well; and he wishes you very much to send him a printed letter, and so does Fanny – and they both rather think they shall answer it.

[Letter to Cassandra, 11 June 1799]

The printed letters came, both sisters taking the time to organize their writing and despatch. Cassandra would send the children letters together with the letter to her sister Jane, Jane then pretending that they had come separately. Evidently the trick worked though the children were suspicious that the 'wafers' that stuck down the paper were rather moist when they opened them. In this exchange of letters we can see the patience that Jane and Cassandra showed the children, a patience and interest that was to last as the children grew up.

The respect that the adults afforded the children is remarkable. This letter is typical:

My dear Anna

We told Mr. B. Lefroy that if the weather did not prevent us, we should certainly come and see you tomorrow, and bring Cassy, trusting to your being so good as to give her dinner about one o'clock . . . but on giving Cassy her choice of the Fair or Wyards, it must be

confessed that she has preferred the former, which we trust will not greatly affront you; – if it does, you may hope that some little Anna hereafter may revenge the insult by a similar preference of an Alton Fair to her cousin Cassy.

[Letter to Anna Lefroy, 29 September 1814]

Little Cassy was then seven years old.

The same measure of respect was offered on more solemn occasions than possible visits to fairs. When Elizabeth Austen, Edward's wife, died in 1808, her two oldest boys, Edward and George, stayed with Jane in Southampton. They were then fourteen and thirteen respectively:

Edward and George came to us soon after seven on Saturday, very well, but very cold, having by choice travelled on the outside, and with no great coat but what Mr. Wise, the coachman, good-naturedly spared them of his, as they sat by his side. They were so much chilled when they arrived, that I was afraid they must have taken cold; but it does not seem at all the case; I never saw them looking better.

. . . Edward has an old black coat, which will

save *his* having a second new one; but I find that black pantaloons are considered by them as necessary, and of course one would not have them made uncomfortable by the want of what is usual on such occasions.

[Letter to Cassandra, 24 October 1808]

Jane's concern that her nephews should not be discomforted at their mother's funeral shows a genuine sympathy and understanding for the adolescent boys. She is equally sympathetic when her two nieces have to go to see a dentist in London:

> The poor Girls & their Teeth! I have not mentioned them yet, but we were a whole hour at Spence's, & Lizzy's were filed and lamented over again & poor Marianne had two taken out after all, the two just beyond the Eye teeth, to make room for those in front.– When her doom was fixed, Fanny Lizzy & I walked into the next room, where we heard each of the two sharp hasty Screams . . .
>
> . . . The little girls' teeth I can suppose in a critical state, but I think he must be a Lover of Teeth & Money & Mischeif to parade about Fannys.– I would not have had him look at mine for a shilling a tooth & double it.– It was a disagreeable hour.

[Letter to Cassandra, 16 September 1813]

Jane's constant concern with her nieces and nephews is shown both in her delight at the babies and her interest in their emergence as young adults. Perhaps the most significant culmination of her good relationship with the

The exterior of Chawton Cottage, where Jane wrote most successfully from her arrival in 1809 until her death in 1817. The cottage is open to the public and contains many mementoes of the family.

The door to Chawton Cottage, where Jane was also visited by her many nephews and nieces, who remembered her as an aunt and not as a writer.

next generation of Austens comes in the correspondence which she has with Fanny, Edward Austen's eldest child, about Fanny's being 'in love'. Here we can see the mature fruition of the continuing affection and right regard begun with 'itty Dordy', developed with 'little Cassy' and enjoyed by the other children in their turn. Fanny, the young woman with whom Jane Austen could giggle as she hurried with a visitor's breeches along the corridors of Godmersham Park when the housemaids had put the gentleman's things in the wrong bedroom, wrote to her aunt telling of her doubts about a man whom she thought she loved. This was Jane's reply:

> Oh! dear Fanny, your mistake has been one that thousands of women fall into. He was the *first* young Man who attached himself to you. That was the charm and most powerful it is . . . Upon the whole, what is to be done? You certainly *have* encouraged him to such a point as to make him feel almost secure of you . . . Oh, my dear Fanny, the more I write about him, the warmer my feelings become, the more strongly I feel the sterling worth of such a young Man & the desirableness of your growing in love with him again . . .
> . . . And now, my dear Fanny, having written so much on one side of the question, I shall turn round & entreat you not to commit yourself farther, & not to think of accepting him unless you really do like him. Anything is to be preferred or endured rather than marrying without Affection.

Fanny was blessed to have such an aunt to confide in and Jane well rewarded by her niece's confidence in her. The letter includes a delightful insight into the subterfuge that Jane indulged, in what she elsewhere referred to as her 'female intelligence':

> Your sending the Music was an admirable device, it made everything easy & I do not know how I would have accounted for the parcel otherwise.
> [Letter to Fanny Knight, 18 November 1814]

Jane has begged Fanny to use some subterfuge in order to keep the correspondence and its contents secret. She had early asked that she should include something in her letters that she, Jane, could read out aloud to the rest of the family whose curiosity would be aroused by the size and number of letters passing between Fanny and herself. Jane Austen was quite as wily as any of her own characters, confessing in another letter that she often resorted to 'a little convenient listening' to find out things that she needed to know.

As it was, in the case of the letters about the young man, the ruse of sending the music worked:

> . . . for though your dear Papa most conscientiously hunted about till he found me alone in the Dining Parlour . . . I do not think anything was suspected.
> [Ibid]

Such an exchange about such a subject speaks volumes about the relationship that Jane Austen was able to establish with her younger relatives.

We can be sure that the niece who said, many years after her death, that 'she seemed to love you, and you loved her in return', spoke for her fellow cousins, as well as for herself.

Chawton House from Prosser's Select Illustrations of Hampshire. *One of the houses that Edward Austen inherited from the Knight family, it seems to have been one of Jane's favourites and she records many visits to it.*

Chawton in Hampshire: 1808-1817

'I have written myself into £250 — which only makes me long for more'

THE SMALL Hampshire village of Chawton, some forty-eight miles from London on the Winchester to Southampton road, is for us in the twentieth century the closest link with Jane Austen. Other than in her novels, it is here that we may come closest to Jane herself. For it was in a 'cottage' in this village that she spent the most eventful, creative and yet at the same time the most serene years of her life. From July 1809 until the summer of 1817 the house now known as *Jane Austen House* was her home, where she lived with her mother, her sister Cassandra and their friend Martha Lloyd. It was in this house that she wrote the majority of her published works, and it was here that her nephews and nieces grew to know their Aunt Jane. The house fortunately still stands, lovingly preserved by the Jane Austen Memorial Trust and furnished as it might have been in her own day. Together with the countryside of Hampshire, Chawton can give us a glimpse of the setting for the last eight years of her life.

It is through her brother Edward that Jane came to live in Chawton. When he inherited the Knight property in Kent, Edward also acquired Chawton Manor and a large portion of the land of the village itself. By 1808, when Jane and her mother were still quite happily living in Southampton, references appear in letters to the 'plan for Chawton'. It appears that Edward offered his mother the choice of a house in Kent or one in Hampshire, either of which she could have rent free for life. On 24th October 1808 Jane is optimistic about the move to Chawton:

> Of Chawton I think I can have nothing more to say but that everything you say about it in the letter now before me will, I am sure, as soon as I am able to read it to her, make my mother consider the plan with more and more pleasure.
>
> [Letter to Cassandra, 24 October 1808]

Jane was right. By November of that year there was news that the house was to have six bedrooms and a room for a servant, and by the following summer the move had been made. In a letter written in verse congratulating her brother Frank on the birth of a son, Jane included a verse announcing their own satisfaction:

> As for ourselves, we're very well;
> As unaffected prose will tell.–
> Cassandra's pen will paint our state,
> The many comforts that await
> Our Chawton home, how much we find
> Already in it, to our mind;
> And how convinced, that when complete
> It will all other Houses beat
> That ever have been made or mended,
> With rooms concise or rooms distended.
> You'll find us very snug next year,
> Perhaps with Charles and Fanny near.
>
> [Letter to Frank Austen, 26 July 1809]

Cassandra summed up the situation when she said years later, 'Thanks to my brother, I shall still be able to occupy the same comfortable cottage at Chawton'. It was only Edward's good fortune that brought the Austen ladies to Chawton and provided for them while they were there.

Perhaps the best description of the cottage is in J. E. Austen Leigh's *Memoir*:

'The house stood in the village of Chawton, about a mile from Alton, on the right hand side, just where the road to Winchester branches off that to Gosport. It was so close to the road that the front door opened upon it; while a very narrow enclosure paled in on either side protected the building from danger of collision with any runaway vehicle. I believe it had originally been built as an inn, for which purpose it was certainly well situated. Afterwards it had been occupied by Mr. Knight's

John Murray, who became Jane Austen's publisher when Emma *appeared. Earlier novels,* Sense and Sensibility, Pride and Prejudice *and* Mansfield Park *had all been previously published by Egerton: 'Mr. Murray's Letter is come. He is a rogue of course, but a civil one. He offers £450 (for* Emma*) but wants to have the copyright of MP and S&S. included. It will end in my publishing for myself I daresay. He sends more praise however than I expected.' (Letter by Jane, 17 October 1815). Murray did in fact publish* Emma. *National Portrait Gallery, London.*

One of the most interesting features of the property today is the wash-house or baking house to be found at the rear of the house. We must not pass it by, for Jane delighted in what she termed 'Experimental House-keeping'. She would as happily bake bread, sew and make wine as she would read and write.

> My mother desires me to tell you that I am a very good housekeeper, which I have no reluctance in doing, because I really think it my peculiar excellence, and for this reason – I always take care to provide such things as please my own appetite, which I consider as the chief merit in housekeeping. I have had some ragout veal, and I mean to have some haricot mutton to-morrow. We are to kill a pig soon.
> [Letter to Cassandra, 17 November 1798]

Austen Leigh is able to give us an eye-witness account of Jane Austen when she lived at Chawton. He remembered her as rather old-fashioned in her ways; she was never seen, either morning or afternoon, without a cap, and Austen Leigh believed that both Jane and Cassandra were thought to have 'taken to the garb of middle age earlier than their years or looks required'.

Chawton House, the Manor House, belonged to Edward, but was lived in until 1812 by a tenant. After this time various members of Jane's family used it, including Edward, and we know that she was a frequent visitor to that fine Tudor house with the church of St Nicholas in its grounds.

The village seemed to suit Jane Austen. It is generally believed that the return to Hampshire (Chawton is only some fifteen miles from Steventon) was more like a home-coming. Certainly the time she spent in this second Hampshire home was to prove the most successful and profitable.

'MY OWN DARLING CHILD'

Critics cannot altogether agree about Jane Austen's methods of writing. It is impossible to know why there are such long gaps in the correspondence with her publishers. Even after Crosby had offered to sell back the manuscript of *Susan* (Northanger Abbey) his offer was not taken up until five years after it was made. Some believe that Jane Austen lost faith in her work, or that she was not satisfied that any of it was in a 'final' form. Others consider that the delay was a blessing as it provided the opportunity for her to perfect each piece. Professor Douglas Jefferson suggests the benefit of the delay:

'Whatever her reasons for waiting the outcome places her in a very special category of novelists. Most novelists have written for immediate publication, whereas some of Jane Austen's novels appeared as much as sixteen years after what is taken to be the earliest version.'

steward; but by some additions to the house, and some judicious planting and screening, it was made a pleasant and commodious abode. Mr. Knight was experienced and adroit at such arrangements, and this was a labour of love to him. A good-sized entrance and two sitting-rooms made the length of the house, all intended originally to look upon the road, but the large drawing room window was blocked up and turned into a bookcase, and another opened at the side which gave to a view only turf and trees, as a high wooden fence and hornbeam hedge shut out the Winchester Road, . . .'

Today the house retains, despite an alteration to part of the roof, something of the character of the improvements that Edward Knight made for his mother and sisters. In particular the garden, which was so carefully tended by Jane's mother, is kept much as it would have been during Jane's stay.

While living at Chawton something, or someone, stirred Jane Austen to set about getting her writing into print. It would appear that it was her brother Henry. In the eight years that she lived in Chawton she made frequent trips to stay with him in London, and it was during these visits that her dealings with publishers took place. It is Henry who is most closely associated with her writing during these years, as it was he who gave away the secret that she was an author.

Jane Austen's own account of her writing, from a list in her own hand, dates the last novels as follows:

> *Mansfield Park*. Begun somewhere about February 1811. Finished soon after June 1813
> *Persuasion*. Begun Augt. 8th 1815. Finished Augt. 6th 1816
> *Emma*. Begun Jany. 21 1814. Finished March 29 1815

These novels represent those which were begun at Chawton as opposed to those which had been written much earlier and since revised or re-written. Cassandra Austen has left us an account of those:

> First Impressions begun in Oct. 1796
> Finished in Augt. 1797. Published afterwards, with alterations & contractions under the Title of Pride & Prejudice.
> Sense and Sensibility begun Nov. 1797
> I am sure that something of this same story and characters had been written earlier & called Elinor and Marianne.
> Mansfield Park, begun somewhere about Feby. 1811 – finished soon after June 1813
> Emma begun Jany. 21st 1814 finished August 1816
> Northanger Abbey was written about the year 98 & 99

It is not clear what it was that helped Jane Austen overcome her earlier disappointment with publishers. All we know is that by Thursday April 25th 1811 she is busy correcting page proofs of *Sense and Sensibility* for Thomas Egerton who was proposing to publish it later in the year. The book was to be published at the author's expense (not an uncommon practice), and it was to be in three volumes. Jane Austen often referred to her books as her 'children', not in a cloyingly sentimental way, but in an amused proprietary fashion. Writing in 1815 to congratulate her niece on the birth of a daughter she writes of her own 'child':

> My Dear Anna:
> As I wish very much to see *your* Jemima I am sure you would like to see my *Emma* . . .
> [Letter to Anna Lefroy, 1815]

While correcting pages of *Sense and Sensibility*, she assured Cassandra that she was never 'too busy to think of S & S. I can no more forget it, than a mother can forget her suckling child'. She was anxious to get the book into print and tells Cassandra that Henry had been hurrying the printer in London. Clearly the whole family was excited about the prospect of publication at last.

Sense and Sensibility was published in November 1811, fourteen years after its earliest version had been written. It was to make Jane Austen £140 (a sum which needs to be multiplied by at least ten times to find today's equivalent). We must not pretend that she did not enjoy the money that she made from her success. She had always considered that single ladies without an income were rather pitiful creatures. Her writing gave her an income and she clearly enjoyed the independence and the satisfaction of being a successful writer. She did not, however, consider herself a 'best selling author'. But while we can appreciate her modest pleasure, we should not overlook her honesty when she talks of the money that she has made:

> You will be glad to hear that every Copy of S. & S. is sold & and that it had brought me £140 besides the Copyright, if that should ever be of any value. – I have written myself into £250 – which only makes me long for more.
> [Letter to Cassandra, 3 July 1813]

The success of *Sense and Sensibility* resulted in *Pride and Prejudice*, the 'lop't and crop't' version of *First Impressions*, which Jane had been writing and revising since 1796, being sold to Egerton, the publisher. For this she was offered £110, which she accepted, with some disappointment; 'I would rather have had £150, but we could not both be pleased'. The kindly aunt was also, it would appear, prepared to become a shrewd business woman. She tells Cassandra that the money for *Pride and Prejudice* would come at the end of the twelvemonth.

Thomas Egerton of the Military Library in Whitehall remained Jane Austen's publisher for the next two books after *Sense and Sensibility*: *Pride and Prejudice* and *Mansfield Park*. Of these it was only *Pride and Prejudice* that he published at his own expense, having bought the work outright. It was his apparent hesitation over a second edition of *Mansfield Park* that led Jane Austen to seek a different publisher. It was then that John Murray took over the publication of her work.

We do not know much about the way that the family received *Sense and Sensibility* apart from the story that one of Jane's nieces saw it at a library but left it there thinking that so silly a title could not possibly belong to a good book.

All of Jane Austen's novels that appeared during her lifetime were published anonymously, merely bearing the legend 'By a Lady'. This was not uncommon, but other evidence suggests that Jane Austen, perhaps more than most women novelists, shunned publicity. She asked her family to keep her authorship a secret, and was not too pleased when Henry let people know that his sister was the author of *Pride and Prejudice* and *Sense und Sensibility*. By 25th September 1813, however, she was resigned to having been found out:

> . . . the truth is the Secret has spread so far as to be scarcely the Shadow of a secret now – & that I believe whenever the third appears, I shall not even attempt to tell Lies about it. – I shall rather try to make all the Money than all the Mystery I can of it. People shall pay for their knowledge if I can make them. – Henry heard P. & P. warmly praised in Scotland . . . & what does he do in the warmth of his Brotherly vanity & love, but immediately tell them who wrote it! A Thing once set going in that way – one knows how it spreads! and he, Dear Creature, has set it going so much more than once.

She goes on to say that she was particularly pleased that Cassandra still kept her secret, and that she was trying to harden herself to being known as an author. In the same letter she remarks that being an author is not, after all, of any real consequence, but is merely a trifle 'in all its Bearings to the really important points of one's existence!'

We should perhaps take note of Jane Austen's reservation. Her novels are indeed only a very small part of her life. Her comment can be a useful antidote to the more usual idea that her life is of little significance compared with her literary output.

Of the publication of *Pride and Prejudice* in January 1813 we know quite a lot. Jane is enthusiastic in her letters to Cassandra, writing to tell her that 'I have got my own darling child from London'. She also relates how she and her mother were reading it aloud to an unsuspecting visitor who found it amusing. By 4th February, the 'readings' to Miss Benn were not going

---

Title pages of the English and American editions of Sense and Sensibility, *Jane's first published work. All her novels were published anonymously. Eventually, however, she was prepared to 'forsake the mystery' in order to concentrate on the 'making of money'. Jane was unashamedly delighted with this aspect of writing. An income meant independence for a single woman in the eighteenth century, who would otherwise have to rely on the benevolence of relations.*

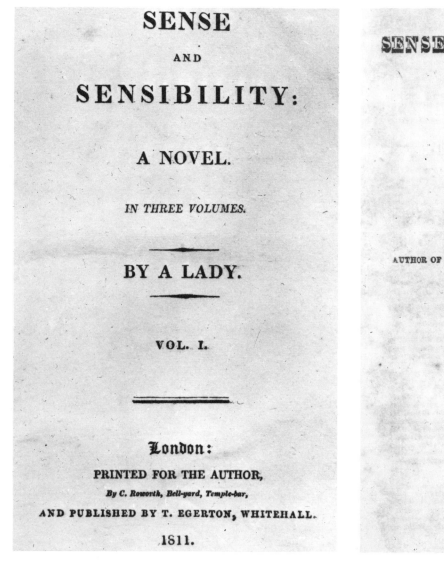

SENSE

AND

SENSIBILITY:

A NOVEL.

IN THREE VOLUMES.

BY A LADY.

VOL. I.

London:
PRINTED FOR THE AUTHOR,
By C. Roworth, Bell-yard, Temple-bar,
AND PUBLISHED BY T. EGERTON, WHITEHALL.
1811.

SENSE AND SENSIBILITY:

A NOVEL.

BY
MISS AUSTEN,
AUTHOR OF "PRIDE AND PREJUDICE," "EMMA," &c. &c.

IN TWO VOLUMES.
VOL. I.

Philadelphia:
CAREY & LEA.
1833.

H.R.H. the Prince of Wales, to whom Jane Austen, at the Prince's own suggestion, dedicated the novel Emma.

of *Sense and Sensibility* and *Pride and Prejudice* were published, the latter within a year of first publication. Once again we find Jane Austen interested in financial as well as artistic considerations:

> Since I wrote last, my second edition has stared me in the face.– Mary tells me that Eliza means to buy it. I wish she may. . . . I cannot help hoping that *many* will feel themselves obliged to buy it. I shall not mind imagining it a disagreeable Duty to them, so as they do it.
>
> [Letter to Cassandra, 6 November 1813]

Once *Sense and Sensibility* was in print, Jane Austen seems to have got into her stride. For the second editions of that and of *Pride and Prejudice* were quickly followed by the first of *Mansfield Park*, in May 1814, at a time when she had already begun *Emma*. From letters we know in quite some detail how these last works were received. Henry, we learn, found *Mansfield Park* very different from the other two but 'does not appear to think it at all inferior'.

A men's fashion plate giving a clear idea of the costume of the day. The 'sculptured' clothes have to be well-cut and displayed by a good figure, and are expensive in both cloth and cut. Bath Reference Library.

too well. Jane confesses that she herself had had some 'fits of disgust' but she cheerfully attributed these to her mother's poor reading for 'though she perfectly understands the characters herself, she cannot speak as they ought'. But in general Jane is well pleased with the work: 'Upon the whole, however, I am quite vain enough and well satisfied enough.'

She goes on to make a lighthearted and playful criticism of the book:

> The work is rather too light and bright, and sparkling; it wants shade; it wants to be stretched out here and there with a long chapter of sense, if it could be had; if not of solemn specious nonsense, about something unconnected with the story; an essay on writing, a critique on Walter Scott, or the history of Buonaparte . . .
>
> [Letter to Cassandra, 4 February 1813]

Jane Austen knew very well that nothing of the kind was needed.

With *Pride and Prejudice* in print, Jane declared that she was now going to write about something quite different: ordination. And this she did in *Mansfield Park*.

In November of the same year (1813) second editions

Of *Mansfield Park* and *Emma* we have a further, more interesting source of information in addition to letters. Jane Austen compiled a collection of 'Opinions of *Mansfield Park*' and did the same for *Emma*. From conversation, letters and hearsay she collected comments and carefully wrote them out herself, thereby providing the first collected criticism of these two works. One or two of the most outstanding comments will serve to convey the range of opinions that she found worth recording. (The full collection of criticisms are available in R. W. Chapman's edition of Jane Austen's *Minor Works*, Oxford 1975.)

Jane's mother '–did not like it so well as P. & P. Thought Fanny Insipid.– enjoyed Mrs. Norris.' Her sister Cassandra 'thought it quite as clever, though not so brilliant as P. & P.–Fond of Fanny.–Delighted much in Mr. Rushworth's stupidity.–'

On the other hand, a Mrs Augusta Bramstone was not amused. She '–owned that she thought S. & S.–and P. & P. downright nonsense, but expected to like MP. better, and having finished the first volume flattered herself that she had got through the worst.' Lady Gordon, on the other hand, wrote this in anticipation of Sir Walter Scott's famous favourable review of *Emma* in 1816: 'In most novels you are amused for the time with a set of Ideal People whom you never think of afterwards or whom you least expect to meet in common life, whereas with Miss A-s works, and especially in MP. you

actually *live* with them, you fancy yourself one of the family; & the scenes are so exactly descriptive, so perfectly natural, that there is scarcely an Incident or conversation, or a person that you are not inclined to imagine you have at one time or other in your Life been a witness to, born a part in, & been acquainted with.' Jane's sailor brother Charles was by no means so sure: 'Charles–did not like it near so well as P. & P.–thought it wanted incident.'

During the years that these novels were being written and produced by the publishers for a very interested public, life at Chawton went on. These were the years when the children visited Chawton and when Jane was to stay both at Godmersham Park and in London with Henry. Although the stays in London must have included visits to the publisher, their purpose was not solely business.

Amused to find herself in solitary state being driven around London in her brother's barouche, Jane allowed herself to enjoy her income. We read of her visits to the theatre, of her shopping expeditions, of her visits to Wedgwood's store, of her going to exhibitions of paintings. Jane Austen the published novelist appears

---

Scene in a draper's shop in London, 1809. The shop is Harding Howell & Co., 89 Pall Mall. Jane would undoubtedly have visited such shops as these when staying with her brother Henry Austen in London.

The Prince of Wales' bound copies of Emma. *It was said that the Prince Regent, whom Jane Austen did not very much admire, was a devotee of her writing, keeping copies of her works in all of his different residences. Royal Library, Windsor Castle.*

to have been a contented woman. Her writing in these years seemed to go well, and culminated in the production of *Emma*, which many consider her masterpiece.

No one knows the complete reason why Jane Austen transferred her work to John Murray, the famous publisher of Albemarle Street. John Murray offered her £450 for the copyrights of *Sense and Sensibility*, together with *Mansfield Park* and *Emma*. But Henry Austen would not let her accept the offer. He made it clear to Murray that his sister had made more money than that out of 'one very moderate edition of *Mansfield Park*' by itself.

Henry Austen became seriously ill at the time that negotiations with Murray were proceeding and we hear of Jane suggesting that the publisher call on her, at her brother's home in Hans Place: 'A short conversation

may perhaps do more than much writing'. Eventually it was agreed that Murray would publish at Jane Austen's expense, and that he would take 10%. While *Emma* was thus finding its way into print, Jane now began on *Persuasion*, which, together with *Northanger Abbey*, would not be published in her lifetime.

Henry's illness, from which he made a good recovery, had an unexpected outcome. The medical man who attended Henry, a Mr Haden, had a medical acquaintance who was one of the Prince Regent's physicians. Through this gentleman, the Prince Regent, who was an admirer of the writings of the 'Lady' who wrote *Pride and Prejudice*, came to know that this 'Lady' was presently in London. Before long Jane Austen was to find herself in correspondence with the Prince Regent's librarian.

The Prince Regent was a great admirer of her writing and he instructed his librarian, a clergyman called Clarke, to invite Jane Austen to Carlton House, his London home on which he had lavished so much money. Through Mr Clarke, the Prince Regent also made it known that he would approve any request that the author's next book might perhaps be dedicated to himself. This left Jane Austen in something of a dilemma, for she did not like the Prince Regent and in no way approved of his morals or his manners, as is evidenced by his behaviour towards his wife:

> I suppose all the world is sitting in judgement upon the Princess of Wales's Letter. Poor woman, I shall support her as long as I can, because she *is* a Woman, & because I hate her Husband.
>
> [Letter to Martha Lloyd, 16 February 1813]

It *was* an honour to be invited to dedicate a book to the Prince Regent, however, and one that it would be difficult to refuse. Writing to John Murray, Jane Austen accepts the Prince Regent's 'request' or invitation:

> The title page must be Emma, Dedicated by Permission to H.R.H. The Prince Regent —and it is my particular wish that one Set should be completed & sent to H.R.H. two or three days before the Work is generally public.
>
> [Letter to Murray, 11 December 1815]

Murray, like all good publishers, was able to point out that Jane Austen had made a mistake in asking for the dedication to go on the title page. Like all good authors Jane Austen was grateful for Murray's help:

> As to my direction about the title page, it was arising from my ignorance only, and my having never noticed the proper placc for a dedication . . . I feel happy in having a friend to save me from the ill effect of my own blunder.
>
> [Letter to Murray, 11 December 1815]

The book was delivered and the Prince Regent delighted with the handsome copy which she sent him. Jane Austen teased Murray when she wrote telling him that the Prince Regent had received his copy safely:

> You will be pleased to hear that I have received the Prince's thanks for the *handsome* copy I sent him of *Emma*. Whatever he may think of *my* share of the work, yours seems to have been quite right.
>
> [Letter to Murray, 1 April 1816]

There is a delightful irony in the dedication of *Emma* to the Prince Regent. The youthful authoress had many times written comical dedications to her very earliest writings. The Prince Regent would have no idea that his was merely the last, though perhaps the most distinguished of a long line of satirical dedications. Here the mature Jane Austen was dedicating one of her finest pieces of work to a man whom she disliked, and who represented in his extravagances and indulgences everything that she abhorred and that her novels held up to ridicule.

Be that as it may, the addition of *Emma* in a specially bound edition bearing the Prince of Wales's Feathers on the spine, to the Royal Library at Windsor must represent a seal upon Jane Austen's success.

Public Acclaim

'The most unlearned and uninformed female who ever dared to be an authoress'

THE REV JAMES STAINER CLARKE, the Prince Regent's librarian, was so enthusiastic about Jane Austen's novels, and the Prince's delight in them, that he allowed himself to suggest ways that she might wish to develop her talent. He rather immodestly suggested that the story of a certain clergyman, clearly himself, ought perhaps to be her next work. He also suggested that she could address herself to the task of writing a historical romance based on the House of Saxe-Coburg.

Jane Austen deftly turned his suggestion aside while conceding that such a serious work would perhaps be much more worthwhile than her 'pictures of domestic life in country villages'. It is only in such infrequent references that we find Jane Austen talking about her writing. Her correspondence with Clarke provides a rare glimpse of the authoress reflecting upon her art:

> I could no more write a romance than an epic poem. I could not sit seriously down to write a serious romance under any other motive than to save my life; and if it were indispensable for me to keep it up and never relax into laughing at myself or other people, I am sure I should be hung before I had finished the first chapter. No, I must keep to my own style and go my own way; and though I may never succeed again in that, I am convinced that I should totally fail in any other.
> [Letter to James Clarke, 1 April 1816]

'Keeping to my own style' and going on in 'my own way' shows the deliberate choice that Jane Austen was making. She knew her own strengths and made no excuse for being a 'comic' writer. It is the fear of breaking out into laughter that precludes her from writing 'seriously'. To Jane Austen everything was a source of amusement; it was the comedy of human affairs that intrigued her.

Little is really known about Jane Austen's methods of composition. Guesses are made that she would use an almanack, and her accurate dating of events and the phases of the moon seem to indicate this. Yet for more general information about the way in which she wrote, we rely more upon family tradition than on any hard evidence. We can be sure that she kept herself busy with her writing, for in the space of only five years she was to produce four major novels.

There are two accounts of her writing handed down in her family, both in their own way rather pleasing. The first is from J. E. Austen Leigh's *Memoir*: 'Most of the work must have been done in the general sitting-room, subject to all kinds of casual interruptions. She was careful that her occupation should not be suspected by servants, or visitors, or any persons beyond

---

A still from the film of Pride and Prejudice *made in 1940 and starring Greer Garson and Laurence Olivier. The men's costume is accurate, the ladies' quite out of period.*

Dec: 11.

Dear Sir

My Emma is now so near publication that I feel it right to assure you of my not having forgotten your kind recommendation of an early copy for C.H. — & that I have Mr. Murray's promise of its being sent to H.R.H. under cover to you, three days previous to the Work being really out. —

I must make use of this opportunity to thank you dear Sir, for the very high praise you bestow on my other Novels — I am too vain to wish to convince you that you have praised them beyond their Merit. —

My greatest anxiety at present is that this 4.th work shd. not disgrace what was good in the others. But on this point I will do myself the justice to declare that whatever may be my wishes for its' success, I am very strongly haunted by the idea that to those Readers who have preferred P&P. it will appear inferior in Wit, & to those who have preferred M.P. very inferior in good Sense. Such as it is however, I hope you will do me the favour of accepting a Copy. Mr. M. will have directions for sending one. I am quite honoured by your thinking me capable of drawing such a Clergyman

A letter in Jane Austen's hand to the Prince of Wales' librarian, the Rev J. Stainer Clarke, in which she tells him that a copy of Emma, *which was dedicated to the Prince Regent, would shortly be sent to the Prince. Jane Austen's House, Chawton.*

her own family party. She wrote upon small sheets of paper which could easily be put away, or covered with a piece of blotting paper. There was, between the front door and the offices, a swing door which creaked when it was opened; but she objected to having this little inconvenience remedied, because it gave her notice when anyone was coming.'

The second account comes from Edward Knight's third daughter, but it is not a first-hand account and cannot be relied upon:
'I remember that when Aunt Jane came to us at Godmersham she used to bring the MS of whatever novel she was writing with her, and would shut herself up with my elder sisters in one of the bedrooms to read them aloud. I and the younger ones used to hear peals of laughter through the door, and thought it very hard that we should be shut out from what was so delightful. I also remember how Aunt Jane would sit quietly working beside the fire in the library, saying nothing for a good while, and then would suddenly burst out laughing, jump up and run across the room to a table where pens and paper were lying, write something down, and then come back to the fire and go on quietly working as before.'

The picture is delightful, but most probably the imagined scene in the memory of someone wishing to be included in 'having known Jane Austen' when she was writing her novels.

On the other hand we do know that Jane Austen shared much of her work with members of her family. She was prepared to answer their questions about people in the stories and gave them the solutions to

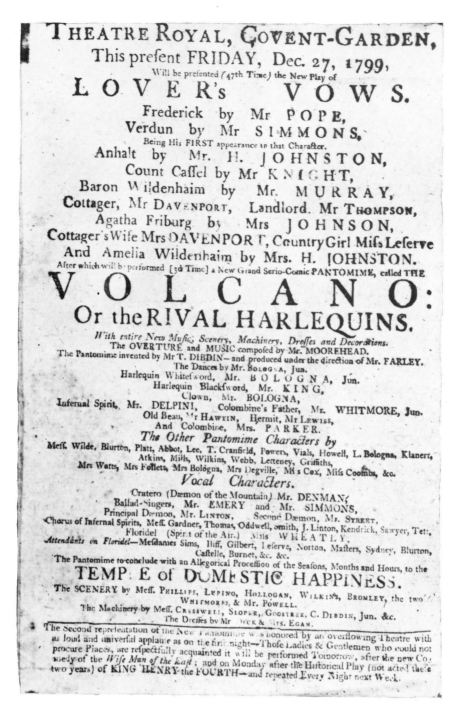

THEATRE ROYAL, COVENT-GARDEN,

This present FRIDAY, Dec. 27, 1799,

Will be presented (47th Time) the New Play of

LOVER's VOWS.

Frederick by Mr POPE,
Verdun by Mr SIMMONS,

Being His FIRST appearance in that Character.

Anhalt by Mr. H. JOHNSTON,
Count Caffel by Mr KNIGHT,
Baron Wildenhaim by Mr. MURRAY,
Cottager, Mr DAVENPORT, Landlord, Mr THOMPSON,
Agatha Friburg by Mrs JOHNSON,
Cottager's Wife Mrs DAVENPORT, Country Girl Mifs Leferve
And Amelia Wildenhaim by Mrs. H. JOHNSTON.

After which will be performed [3d Time] a New Grand Serio-Comic PANTOMIME, called THE

VOLCANO:

Or the RIVAL HARLEQUINS.

With entire New Mufic, Scenery, Machinery, Dreffes and Decorations.
The OVERTURE and MUSIC composed by Mr. MOOREHEAD.
The Pantomime invented by Mr T. DIBDIN—and produced under the direction of Mr. FARLEY.
The Dances by Mr. BOLOGNA, Jun.
Harlequin Whitefword, Mr. BOLOGNA, Jun.
Harlequin Blackfword, Mr. KING,
Clown, Mr. BOLOGNA,
Infernal Spirit, Mr. DELPINI, Colombine's Father, Mr. WHITMORE, Jun.
Old Beau, Mr HAWTIN, Hermit, Mr LEWISS,
And Colombine, Mrs. PARKER.
The Other Pantomime Characters by
Meff. Wilde, Blurton, Platt, Abbot, Lee, T. Cranfield, Powers, Vials, Howell, L. Bologna, Klanert,
Atkins, Mills, Wilkins, Webb, Letteney, Griffiths,
Mrs Watts, Mrs Follett, Mrs Bologna, Mrs Degville, Mifs Cox, Mifs Coombs, &c.
Vocal Characters.
Cratero (Dæmon of the Mountain) Mr. DENMAN,
Ballad-Singers, Mr. EMERY and Mr. SIMMONS,
Principal Dæmon, Mr. LINTON, Second Dæmon, Mr. STREET,
Chorus of Infernal Spirits, Meff. Gardner, Thomas, Oddwell, smith, J. Linton, Kendrick, Sawyer, Tett,
Floridel (Spirit of the Air.) Mifs WHEATLY.
Attendants on Floridel—Mefdames Sims, Iliff, Gilbert, Leferve, Norton, Masters, Sydney, Blurton,
Caftelle, Burnet, &c. &c.
The Pantomime to conclude with an Allegorical Proceffion of the Seafons, Months and Hours, to the

TEMPLE of DOMESTIC HAPPINESS.

The SCENERY by Meff. PHILLIPS, LUPINO, HOLLOGAN, WILKINS, BROMLEY, the two
WHITMORES, & Mr. POWELL.
The Machinery by Meff. CRESSWELL, SLOPER, GOOSTREE, C. DIBDIN, Jun. &c.
The Dreffes by Mr DICK & Mrs. EGAN.

The Second reprefentation of the New Pantomime was honored by an overflowing Theatre with
as loud and univerfal applaufe as on the firft night—Thofe Ladies & Gentlemen who could not
procure Places, are refpectfully acquainted it will be performed Tomorrow, after the new Comedy of the Wife Man of the Laft; and on Monday after the Hiftorical Play (not acted thefe
two years) of KING HENRY the FOURTH—and repeated Every Night next Week.

Playbill for Lover's Vows, *the subject of amateur theatricals in* Mansfield Park. *Jane Austen was a frequent theatre-goer, recording many visits there in London, Southampton and Bath. Jane Austen's House, Chawton.*

several of the puzzles that the novels contain. Jane's nephew James writes:

'. . . we learned that Miss Steele never succeeded in catching the Doctor; that Kitty Bennet was satisfactorily married to a clergyman . . . that Mr. Woodhouse survived his daughter's marriage and kept her and Mr. Knightley from settling at Donwell, about two years; and that the letters placed by Frank Churchill before Jane Fairfax, which she swept away unread, contained the word 'pardon'.'

Jane Austen 'allowed' her characters their own life and while she would sometimes humour her family by telling them more than was in the novels, she could also shrink from venturing to know. When her niece Fanny wrote an imaginary letter from Elizabeth to Georgina Darcy, and sent it to her Aunt, Jane replied that she very much enjoyed the letter but could not pretend to answer it:

> Even had I more time, I should not feel at all sure of the sort of letter that Miss D. would write.
> [Letter to Cassandra, 24 May 1813]

She might 'look' for her characters in real paintings which were on exhibition in London, and sometimes appear to find them:

Henry and I went to the Exhibition in Spring Gardens ... I was very well pleased –particularly with a small portrait of Mrs. Bingley, [Jane Bennet of *Pride & Prejudice*] excessively like her. I went in hopes of seeing one of her Sister, but there was no Mrs. Darcy ... Mrs. Bingley's is exactly herself, size, shaped face, features and sweetness; there never was a greater likeness. She is dressed in a white gown, with green ornaments, which convinces me of what I had always supposed, that green was a favourite colour with her.
[Letter to Cassandra, 24 May 1813]

Yet despite these imagined visual representations in art, Jane Austen's characters lived for her alone. She scorned the idea that they were based upon people whom she had met. She claimed that she was far too proud of her gentlemen for them to be merely people that she knew.

Jane's correspondence gives all too few glimpses of the authoress at work. A group of letters to her nieces in 1814, where she is offering them advice about their writing, are the closest we get. Here she shows herself to be passionately concerned with accuracy and attention to detail:

A few verbal corrections were all I felt tempted to make–the principal of them is a speech of St. Julian's to Lady Helena–which you see I have presumed to alter.–as Lady H. is Cecilia's superior, it would not be correct to talk of *her* being introduced: Cecilia must be the person introduced–and I do not like a Lover's speaking in the 3rd person; it's too much like the formal part of Lord Orville, & I think is not natural.
[Letter to Anna Austen, May or June 1814]

In another letter to Anna she is more forthright:

Devereaux Forester's being ruined by his Vanity is extremely good; but I wish you would not let him plunge into a 'vortex of Dissipation.' I do not object to the Thing, but I cannot bear the expression; it is such

A finely illustrated 1833 edition of Emma.

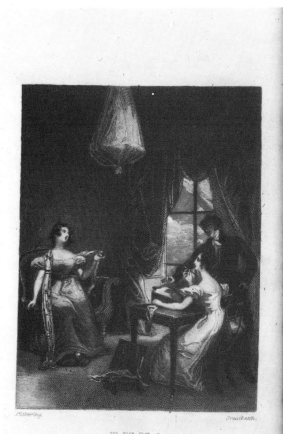

EMMA.

There was no being displeased with such an encourager, for his admiration made him discern a likeness before it was possible.

London, Published by Richard Bentley, 1833.

EMMA,
A NOVEL.
BY
JANE AUSTEN.

Tell me, then, have I no chance of succeeding?

LONDON:
RICHARD BENTLEY,
SUCCESSOR TO H. COLBURN,
CUMMING, DUBLIN.–BELL & BRADFUTE, EDINBURGH.
GALIGNANI, PARIS.
1833.

A London street on a windy day. A scene that underlines the impracticability of fashion in the late eighteenth century. Dress was for display, not for day-to-day wear. Victoria and Albert Museum, London.

thorough novel slang—and so old, that I dare say Adam met with it in the first novel he opened.

[Letter to Anna, 28 September 1814]

After many compliments about Anna's writing, Aunt Jane can be quite harsh about detail:

Lyme will not do, Lyme is towards 40 miles distance from Dawlish & would not be talked of there.—I have put Starcross instead . . .

and again:

. . . I have scratched out Sir Thomas from walking with the other Men to the Stables &c the very day after breaking his arm—for though I find your Papa *did* walk out immediately after *his* arm was set, I think it can be so little used as to *appear* unnatural in a book . . .

. . . They must be *two* days going from Dawlish to Bath; they are nearly 100 miles apart.

[Letter to Anna, 10 August 1814]

The advice is helpful and underlines the need for careful research.

But in whatever way she wrote Jane Austen leaves us in no doubt at all as to her enjoyment of the sales of her books:

Rowlandson's cartoon of the 'Great Exhibition Room at Somerset House'. Jane Austen tells how she attended art exhibitions and sought out pictures that she could imagine were portraits of the characters in her novels, sometimes finding likenesses to her satisfaction.

People are more ready to borrow and praise, than to buy—which I cannot wonder at; but though I like praise as well as anybody, I like what Edward calls *Pewter* too.

[Letter to Fanny Knight, 30 November 1814]

As long as people bought her books she was happy. Her collection of opinions of *Emma* cheerfully records as many grumbles as commendations:

My Mother: thought it more entertaining than MP.—but not so interesting as P & P—No characters to equal Ly Catherine and Mr. Collins. Mrs. Digweed—did not like it so well as the others, in fact if she had not known the Author, could hardly have got through it.— Mr. Fowle—read only the first and last Chapters, because he had heard it was not interesting.

Mr. Jeffery [of the Edinburgh Review] was kept up by it three nights.

The novels were noticed by critics during Jane Austen's lifetime. An unsigned review of *Sense and Sensibility* appeared in the *Critical Review* of November 1811:

'We are no enemies to novels or novel writers, but we regret, that in the multiplicity of them, there are so few worthy of any particular commendation . . . *Sense & Sensibility* is one amongst the few . . . It is well written; the characters are in genteel life, naturally drawn, and judiciously supported. The incidents are probable and highly pleasing, and interesting . . .'

It is probable that Jane would have seen this very favourable review of her 'first own darling child'.

The review of *Pride and Prejudice*, also unsigned, in the *British Critic* of January 1813 was equally favourable, declaring that it was:

'. . . far superior to almost all the publications of the kind which have lately come before us. It has a very unexceptional tendency, the story is well told, the characters remarkably well drawn and supported and written with great spirit as well as vigour.'

But it was Walter Scott's review in the *Quarterly Review*, again unsigned, that did most to signal Jane Austen's arrival in the history of English literature. It is impossible to know whether Jane Austen realized that Scott was the author of this review. It would have pleased her if she had for she had once exclaimed that Walter Scott had no right to be a novelist, that he ought to have been content with being a poet and not taken the bread out of other people's mouths by writing novels.

Scott wrote an extended piece praising *Sense and Sensibility*, *Pride and Prejudice* as well as *Emma*. We know that Jane Austen read the review for she was surprised that there was no mention of *Mansfield Park* anywhere in it. Scott's praise was high, likening her writing to the Flemish School of painting:

> The subjects are often not elegant, and certainly never grand; but they are finished up to nature, and with a precision that delights the reader.

For Sir Walter Scott the anonymous author of these novels was a writer of the highest calibre. Scott's judgement was not at fault.

An endearing reviewer in the *Gentleman's Magazine* of September 1816 was able to assure the public that *Emma* was:

'amusing, if not instructive; and has no tendency to deteriorate the heart.'

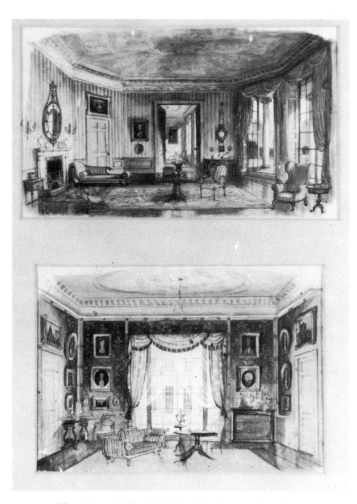

The design by Rex Whistler for a stage adaptation of
Pride and Prejudice *in the 1930s.*

The Final Year

'I am now really a very genteel, portable sort of an Invalid'

JANE AUSTEN died after about a year's illness on July 18th 1817 from a disease the true nature of which remains something of a mystery. She was in her forty-second year.

January of that year saw her writing to that young 'puss Little Cassy', with her characteristic patience and sense of fun, as follows:

Ym raed Yssac

I hsiw uoy a yppah wen raey. Ruoy xis snisuoc emac ereh yadretsey, dna dah hcae a eceip fo ekac. Siht si Yssac's yadhtrib, dna ehs si eerht sraey dlo . . .

The painstaking and delightful aunt signs herself:

Ruoy Etanoitceffa Tnua

Enaj Netsua

Notwahc, Naj. 8.

[Letter to Cassandra, 8 January 1817]

Gradually as the year 1817 progresses Jane Austen's letters betray the deterioration of her health despite her valiant attempt to raise her own spirits and those of her family:

I certainly have not been well for many weeks, and about a week ago I was very poorly, I have had a good deal of fever at times & indifferent nights, but am considerably better now, and recovering my looks a little, which have been bad enough, black and white and every wrong colour. I must not depend on ever blooming again. Sickness is a dangerous Indulgence at my time of life.

[Letter to Caroline Austen, 14 March 1817]

Of this period her brother Henry was later to recall that her 'decline was at first deceitfully slow'. The letters show her rallying from time to time, but they also chronicle what Henry called a 'deep and incurable' decay. By March her latest piece of writing, the early version of what we now call *Sanditon*, but which Jane

Austen called *Catherine*, was, in her own words 'put on the shelve for the present'. To which the sick authoress adds: 'and I don't know that she will ever come out'.

By this time Jane Austen had difficulty in walking and she writes optimistically about a 'scheme' that she has for 'accomplishing more'. She intended to have a saddle made for the donkey, which normally pulled the donkey-cart (still preserved at the house in Chawton), and on which she would ride as a means of getting about and taking exercise. On March 26th she is able to report on her first ride, cheerfully telling her niece Caroline that she enjoyed it very much. But the optimism wears thin, for she continues by admitting that she is 'a poor Honey at present'.

The house in Winchester where Jane Austen stayed during her fatal illness in 1817. It was in this house that Cassandra nursed her, and from it that her coffin was carried to the cathedral for burial.

Throughout this final illness Jane Austen showed courage and good humour. She is constantly praising the nursing that she has, and in describing her ride on her donkey gives us a clear picture of the scene:

> I went up Mounters Lane & round by where the new Cottages are to be, & found the exercise and everything very pleasant, and I had the advantage of agreeable companions, as At. Cass: and Edward [her nephew] walked by my side.– At. Cass. is such an excellent Nurse, so assiduous & unwearied.
>
> [Letter to Fanny Knight, 23 March 1817]

By April she became worse. Ill as she was, the news that her mother had been, for whatever reason, left out of her uncle Mr Leigh Perrot's will, the main hope for security in their old age, depressed her badly. All her life Jane Austen had feared being poor, as she had feared the plight of the single woman without means. Weakened by her illness she evidently succumbed to some kind of depression, for in a letter to her brother Charles, we find her making the effort not only to make amends but to confess her uncharacteristic failing:

The north front of Winchester Cathedral. Cassandra Austen records her sister as having an especial love of this cathedral, and was hence especially pleased when she could be buried here.

> A few days ago my complaint appeared removed, but I am ashamed to say that the shock of my Uncle's will brought on a relapse, & I was so ill on Friday & thought myself so likely to be worse that I could not but press for Cassandra's returning with Frank after the Funeral last night.
>
> [Letter to Charles Austen, 6 April 1817]

From the letters that survive from this period it is easy, with hindsight, to follow the stages in deterioration that are taking place. She always appears hopeful, and eager to make others so too. But she ends Charles's letter by admitting that she is not strong enough to go anywhere unless it be by Hackney Chariot all the way. By April 13th she is confined to bed being only allowed 'removals to a Sopha'; and yet she remained cheerful: '*Now*, I am getting well again, . . . I can sit up in my bed and employ myself.'.

At this point in her illness a physician from Winchester, a Mr Lyford, had been called in by the Alton apothecary and it was considered advisable for Jane Austen to be taken to Winchester to be cared for under Mr Lyford's supervision. Jane wrote to a friend telling her of the plan and praising the care taken of her by her sister Cassandra and her family.

Even at this stage in her very serious illness Jane Austen is able to jest about herself:

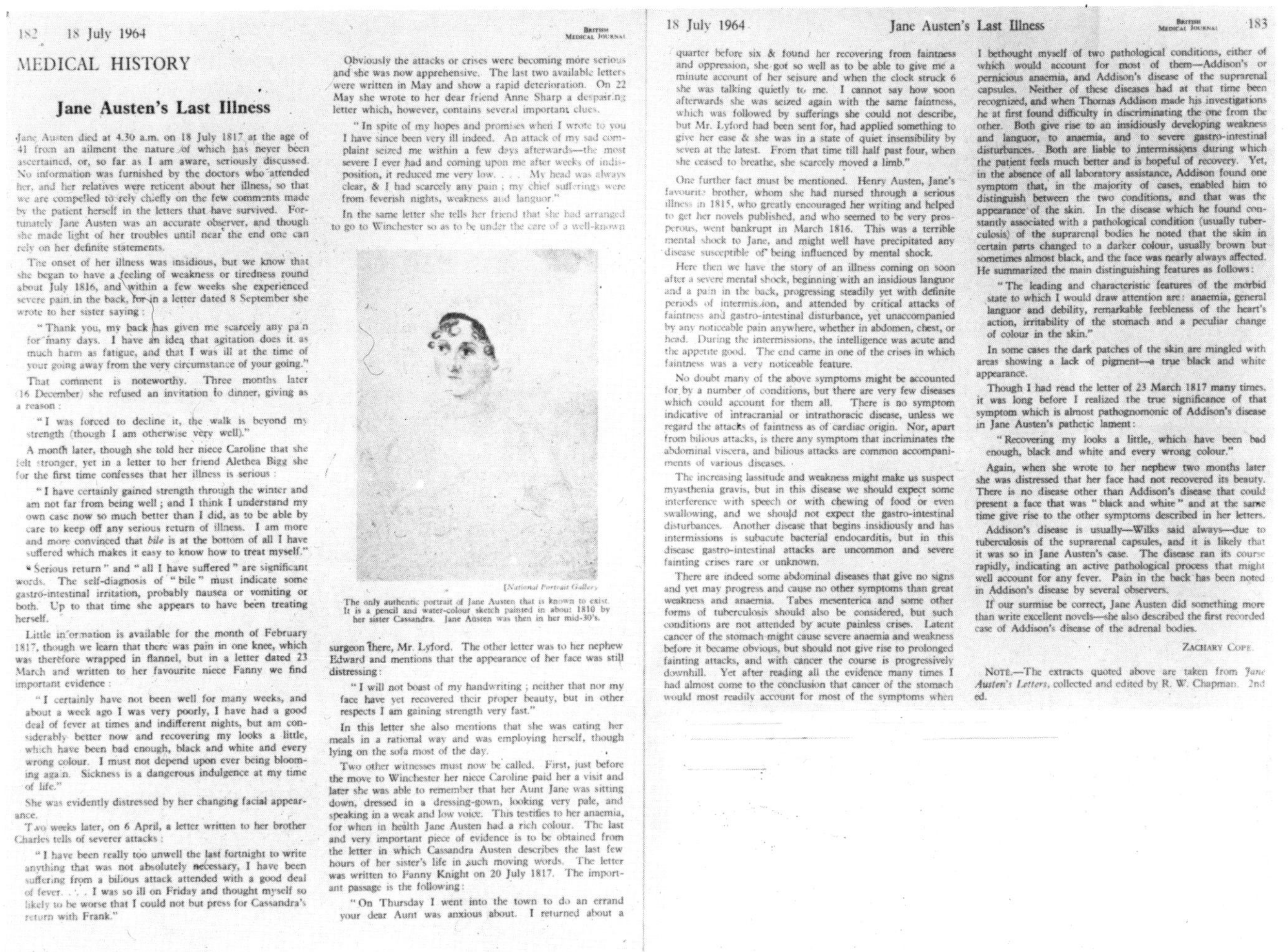

182 18 July 1964 BRITISH MEDICAL JOURNAL

MEDICAL HISTORY

Jane Austen's Last Illness

Jane Austen died at 4.30 a.m. on 18 July 1817 at the age of 41 from an ailment the nature of which has never been ascertained, or, so far as I am aware, seriously discussed. No information was furnished by the doctors who attended her, and her relatives were reticent about her illness, so that we are compelled to rely chiefly on the few comments made by the patient herself in the letters that have survived. Fortunately Jane Austen was an accurate observer, and though she made light of her troubles until near the end one can rely on her definite statements.

The onset of her illness was insidious, but we know that she began to have a feeling of weakness or tiredness round about July 1816, and within a few weeks she experienced severe pain in the back, for in a letter dated 8 September she wrote to her sister saying:

"Thank you, my back has given me scarcely any pain for many days. I have an idea that agitation does it as much harm as fatigue, and that I was ill at the time of your going away from the very circumstance of your going."

That comment is noteworthy. Three months later (16 December) she refused an invitation to dinner, giving as a reason:

"I was forced to decline it, the walk is beyond my strength (though I am otherwise very well)."

A month later, though she told her niece Caroline that she felt stronger, yet in a letter to her friend Alethea Bigg she for the first time confesses that her illness is serious:

"I have certainly gained strength through the winter and am not far from being well; and I think I understand my own case now so much better than I did, as to be able by care to keep off any serious return of illness. I am more and more convinced that *bile* is at the bottom of all I have suffered which makes it easy to know how to treat myself."

"Serious return" and "all I have suffered" are significant words. The self-diagnosis of "bile" must indicate some gastro-intestinal irritation, probably nausea or vomiting or both. Up to that time she appears to have been treating herself.

Little information is available for the month of February 1817, though we learn that there was pain in one knee, which was therefore wrapped in flannel, but in a letter dated 23 March and written to her favourite niece Fanny we find important evidence:

"I certainly have not been well for many weeks, and about a week ago I was very poorly, I have had a good deal of fever at times and indifferent nights, but am considerably better now and recovering my looks a little, which have been bad enough, black and white and every wrong colour. I must not depend upon ever being blooming again. Sickness is a dangerous indulgence at my time of life."

She was evidently distressed by her changing facial appearance.

Two weeks later, on 6 April, a letter written to her brother Charles tells of severer attacks:

"I have been really too unwell the last fortnight to write anything that was not absolutely necessary, I have been suffering from a bilious attack attended with a good deal of fever. . . . I was so ill on Friday and thought myself so likely to be worse that I could not but press for Cassandra's return with Frank."

Obviously the attacks or crises were becoming more serious and she was now apprehensive. The last two available letters were written in May and show a rapid deterioration. On 22 May she wrote to her dear friend Anne Sharp a despairing letter which, however, contains several important clues.

"In spite of my hopes and promises when I wrote to you I have since been very ill indeed. An attack of my sad complaint seized me within a few days afterwards—the most severe I ever had and coming upon me after weeks of indisposition, it reduced me very low. . . . My head was always clear, & I had scarcely any pain; my chief sufferings were from feverish nights, weakness and languor."

In the same letter she tells her friend that she had arranged to go to Winchester so as to be under the care of a well-known

[National Portrait Gallery

The only authentic portrait of Jane Austen that is known to exist. It is a pencil and water-colour sketch painted in about 1810 by her sister Cassandra. Jane Austen was then in her mid-30's.

surgeon there, Mr. Lyford. The other letter was to her nephew Edward and mentions that the appearance of her face was still distressing:

"I will not boast of my handwriting; neither that nor my face have yet recovered their proper beauty, but in other respects I am gaining strength very fast."

In this letter she also mentions that she was eating her meals in a rational way and was employing herself, though lying on the sofa most of the day.

Two other witnesses must now be called. First, just before the move to Winchester her niece Caroline paid her a visit and later she was able to remember that her Aunt Jane was sitting down, dressed in a dressing-gown, looking very pale, and speaking in a weak and low voice. This testifies to her anaemia, for when in health Jane Austen had a rich colour. The last and very important piece of evidence is to be obtained from the letter in which Cassandra Austen describes the last few hours of her sister's life in such moving words. The letter was written to Fanny Knight on 20 July 1817. The important passage is the following:

"On Thursday I went into the town to do an errand your dear Aunt was anxious about. I returned about a

18 July 1964 Jane Austen's Last Illness BRITISH MEDICAL JOURNAL 183

quarter before six & found her recovering from faintness and oppression, she got so well as to be able to give me a minute account of her seisure and when the clock struck 6 she was talking quietly to me. I cannot say how soon afterwards she was seized again with the same faintness, which was followed by sufferings she could not describe, but Mr. Lyford had been sent for, had applied something to give her ease & she was in a state of quiet insensibility by seven at the latest. From that time till half past four, when she ceased to breathe, she scarcely moved a limb."

One further fact must be mentioned. Henry Austen, Jane's favourite brother, whom she had nursed through a serious illness in 1815, who greatly encouraged her writing and helped to get her novels published, and who seemed to be very prosperous, went bankrupt in March 1816. This was a terrible mental shock to Jane, and might well have precipitated any disease susceptible of being influenced by mental shock.

Here then we have the story of an illness coming on soon after a severe mental shock, beginning with an insidious languor and a pain in the back, progressing steadily yet with definite periods of intermission, and attended by critical attacks of faintness and gastro-intestinal disturbance, yet unaccompanied by any noticeable pain anywhere, whether in abdomen, chest, or head. During the intermissions, the intelligence was acute and the appetite good. The end came in one of the crises in which faintness was a very noticeable feature.

No doubt many of the above symptoms might be accounted for by a number of conditions, but there are very few diseases which could account for them all. There is no symptom indicative of intracranial or intrathoracic disease, unless we regard the attacks of faintness as of cardiac origin. Nor, apart from bilious attacks, is there any symptom that incriminates the abdominal viscera, and bilious attacks are common accompaniments of various diseases.

The increasing lassitude and weakness might make us suspect myasthenia gravis, but in this disease we should expect some interference with speech or with chewing of food or even swallowing, and we should not expect the gastro-intestinal disturbances. Another disease that begins insidiously and has intermissions is subacute bacterial endocarditis, but in this disease gastro-intestinal attacks are uncommon and severe fainting crises rare or unknown.

There are indeed some abdominal diseases that give no signs and yet may progress and cause no other symptoms than great weakness and anaemia. Tabes mesenterica and some other forms of tuberculosis should also be considered, but such conditions are not attended by acute painless crises. Latent cancer of the stomach might cause severe anaemia and weakness before it became obvious, but should not give rise to prolonged fainting attacks, and with cancer the course is progressively downhill. Yet after reading all the evidence many times I had almost come to the conclusion that cancer of the stomach would most readily account for most of the symptoms when I bethought myself of two pathological conditions, either of which would account for most of them—Addison's or pernicious anaemia, and Addison's disease of the suprarenal capsules. Neither of these diseases had at that time been recognized, and when Thomas Addison made his investigations he at first found difficulty in discriminating the one from the other. Both give rise to an insidiously developing weakness and languor, to anaemia, and to severe gastro-intestinal disturbances. Both are liable to intermissions during which the patient feels much better and is hopeful of recovery. Yet, in the absence of all laboratory assistance, Addison found one symptom that, in the majority of cases, enabled him to distinguish between the two conditions, and that was the appearance of the skin. In the disease which he found constantly associated with a pathological condition (usually tuberculosis) of the suprarenal bodies he noted that the skin in certain parts changed to a darker colour, usually brown but sometimes almost black, and the face was nearly always affected. He summarized the main distinguishing features as follows:

"The leading and characteristic features of the morbid state to which I would draw attention are: anaemia, general languor and debility, remarkable feebleness of the heart's action, irritability of the stomach and a peculiar change of colour in the skin."

In some cases the dark patches of the skin are mingled with areas showing a lack of pigment—a true black and white appearance.

Though I had read the letter of 23 March 1817 many times, it was long before I realized the true significance of that symptom which is almost pathognomonic of Addison's disease in Jane Austen's pathetic lament:

"Recovering my looks a little, which have been bad enough, black and white and every wrong colour."

Again, when she wrote to her nephew two months later she was distressed that her face had not recovered its beauty. There is no disease other than Addison's disease that could present a face that was "black and white" and at the same time give rise to the other symptoms described in her letters.

Addison's disease is usually—Wilks said always—due to tuberculosis of the suprarenal capsules, and it is likely that it was so in Jane Austen's case. The disease ran its course rapidly, indicating an active pathological process that might well account for any fever. Pain in the back has been noted in Addison's disease by several observers.

If our surmise be correct, Jane Austen did something more than write excellent novels—she also described the first recorded case of Addison's disease of the adrenal bodies.

ZACHARY COPE.

NOTE.—The extracts quoted above are taken from *Jane Austen's Letters*, collected and edited by R. W. Chapman. 2nd ed.

An extract from the British Medical Journal *which explores the nature of Jane Austen's final illness, now believed to have been Addison's Disease.*

> Mrs F.A. [her brother Frank's wife] has had a much shorter confinement than I have–with a Baby to produce into the bargain. We were put to bed nearly at the same time, & she has been quite recovered this great while. . . .
>
> . . . I have not mentioned my dear Mother; she suffered much for me when I was at the worst, . . . In short, if I live to be an old Woman, I must expect to wish I had died now; blessed in the tenderness of such a Family, & before I had survived either them or their affection . . .'
>
> [Letter to Anne Sharp, 22 May 1817]

The move to Winchester, sixteen miles away, took place. Her brother James, rector at Steventon, sent his carriage to convey the now very weak sister to Mrs David's house in College Street. Her brother Henry and her nephew William Knight rode on horseback alongside the coach, and Jane writes to her niece:

> Thanks to the kindness of your Father and Mother in sending me their carriage, my journey hither on Saturday was performed with very little fatigue, and had it been a fine day I think I should have felt none, but it distressed me to see uncle Henry & Wm Knight–who kindly attended us on horseback, riding in rain almost all the way.
>
> [Letter to J. E. Austen, 27 May 1817]

Here, indeed, one sees the tenderness of the Austen family in action. The carriage of one brother conveys the ailing and the nursing sisters, accompanied by another brother and a nephew riding horseback in the rain.

Jane Austen's ending to the letter to her other nephew, whose parents had sent their carriage, is heartbreaking in its humility:

> If ever you are ill, may you be as tenderly nursed as I have been, may the same Blessed alleviations of anxious, simpathising friends be yours, & may you possess–as I dare say you will–the greatest blessing of all, in the consciousness of not being unworthy of their Love. *I* could not feel this.
>
> [Letter to J. E. Austen, 27 May 1817]

At the very end of her illness she remained hopeful, believing that she was improving:

> I live chiefly on the sofa, but am allowed to walk from one room to another. I have been out in a sedan-chair, and am to repeat it, and be promoted to a wheel-chair as the weather serves.

The woman who loved dancing, and who excelled at it, is reduced to looking forward, in her forty-second year, to being promoted to a wheel-chair. While she could hold a pen, so her brother Henry tells us, she kept her correspondence in order, when she could no more hold a pen, she continued with a pencil. In one of the last letters that she was ever to write she is still thinking of her good fortune:

> ... my dearest sister, my tender, watchful, indefatigable nurse, has not been made ill by her exertions. As to what I owe her, and to the anxious affection of all my beloved family on this occasion, I can only cry over it, and pray God to bless them more and more.

[Original untraced but quoted by Henry Austen in his biographical notice of his sister, 1818]

Jane Austen died peacefully in her sister's arms on 18th July 1817. This is Cassandra's account of her death:

> ... till half past four, when she ceased to breathe, she scarcely moved a limb ... A slight motion of the head with evry breath remained till almost the last. I sat close to her with a pillow on my lap to assist in supporting her head, which was almost off the bed, for six hours, – fatigue made me then resign my place to Mrs. J.A. for two hours and a half when I took it again & in about one hour more she breathed her last. I was able to close her eyes myself & it was a great gratification to me to render her these last services.

[Letter to Fanny Knight, July 1817]

Cassandra's grief speaks for Jane Austen's entire family:

> I *have* lost a treasure, such a Sister, such a friend as never can have been surpassed. – she was the sun of my life, the gilder of every pleasure, the soother of every sorrow, I had not a thought concealed from her, & it is as if I had lost a part of myself. I loved her only too well, not better than she deserved ...

[Letter to Fanny Knight, July 1817]

James Austen Leigh, the boy of nine at Jane Austen's funeral in Winchester Cathedral, whose father had lent the carriage to take the sick Jane Austen from Chawton to her lodgings in College Street, ends her story: 'When the end at last came, she sank rapidly, and on being asked by her attendants whether there was anything that she wanted, her reply was '*Nothing but Death*'. In quietness and peace she breathed her last on the morning of July 18, 1817.

On the 24th of that month she was buried in Winchester Cathedral, near the centre of the north aisle, almost opposite to the beautiful chantry tomb of William of Wykham. A large slab of black marble in the pavement marks the place. Her own family only attended the funeral. Her sister returned to her desolated home, there to devote herself for ten years to the care of her aged mother; and to live much in the memory of her lost sister, . . .' [Memoir, Chapter XI]

Cassandra must have the last word. Writing to Fanny Knight, Jane's favourite niece, she described the day of the funeral:

> Thursday was not so dreadful a day to me as you imagined. There was so much necessary to be done that there was no time for additional misery. Everything was conducted with the greatest tranquility, and, but that I was determined I would see the last, and therefore was upon the listen, I should not have known when they left the house. I watched the little mournful procession the length of the street; and when it turned from my sight, and I had lost her for ever, even then I was not overpowered, nor so much agitated as I am now in writing of it. Never was human being more sincerely mourned by those who attended her remains than was this dear creature.

[Letter to Fanny Knight, 29 July 1817]

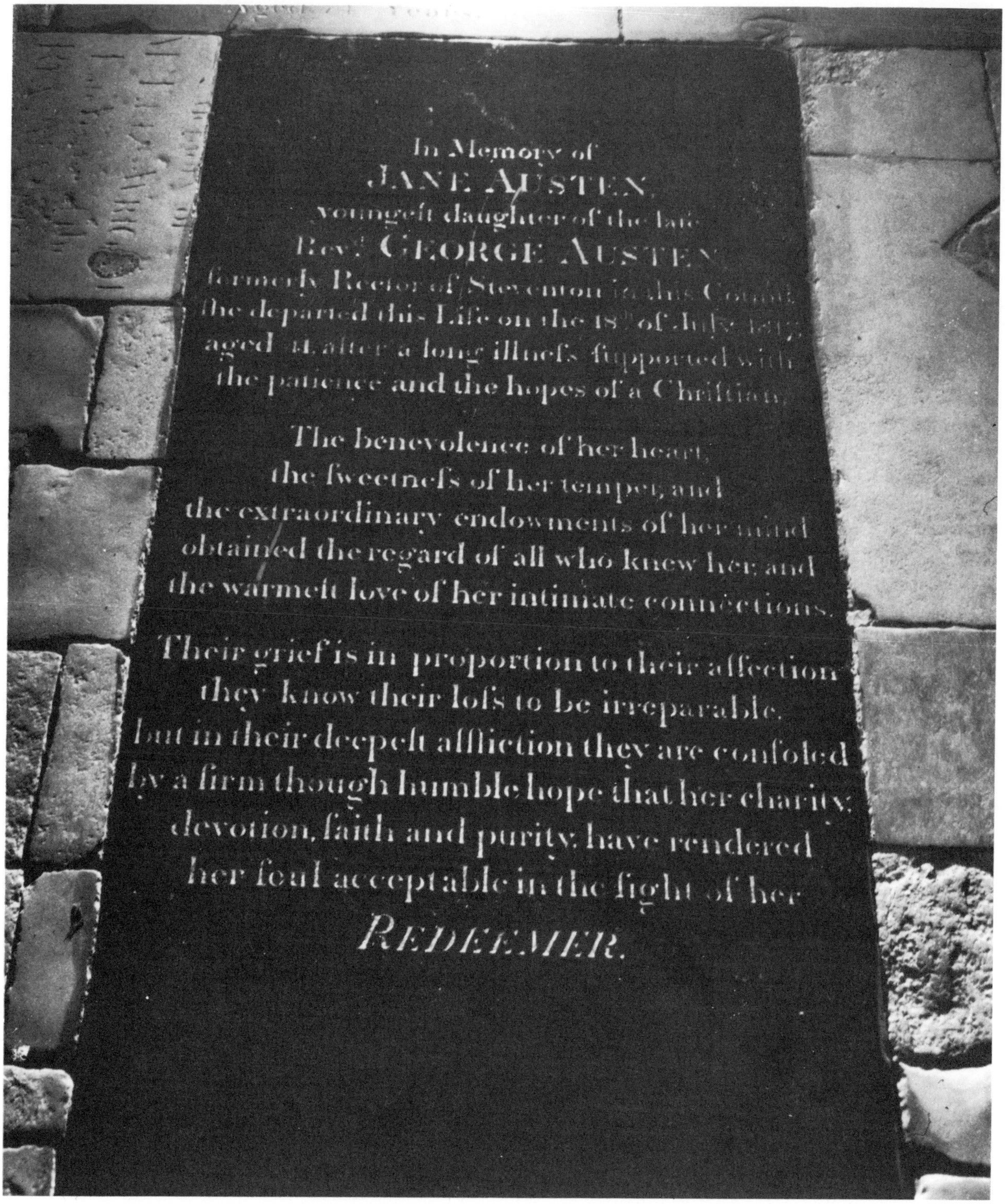

Jane Austen's grave in Winchester Cathedral.

Acknowledgments

The illustrations on pages 32, 38 bottom, 87 and 128 are Crown Copyright, and those on pages 32 and 128 are reproduced by Gracious Permission of Her Majesty the Queen.

The illustrations on pages 26 and 102 are reproduced by kind permission of the President and Fellows of St. John's College, Oxford and those on pages 138 and 141 by permission of the Dean and Chapter of Winchester Cathedral.

A complete facsimile of the Sanditon manuscript in King's College Library, Cambridge was published in 1975 by the Oxford University Press in association with the Scolar Press.

Sources of colour illustrations
J. Butler-Kearney, Alton 57 top; The Cooper-Bridgeman Library, London 57 bottom; Hamlyn Group Picture Library 56; Hamlyn Group–Derek Balmer 52 bottom, 60 left and right, 100 bottom; Hamlyn Group–J. Butler-Kearney 61, 101, 104, 105 top and bottom, 112 top and bottom; King's College, Cambridge–Edward Leigh 108 bottom; The Mansell Collection, London 52 top, 100 top, 108 top, 109; National Portrait Gallery, London 49; The National Trust, London 53; Sunday Times, London 64.

Sources of black and white illustrations
Aerofilms, Boreham Wood 83; Bath Reference Library 88, 90 top, 95; Birmingham Museums and Art Gallery 84 top; The Bodleian Library, Oxford 41 top left; J. Butler-Kearney, Alton 17 top, 18 bottom, 25 top right, 43 top and bottom, 103 top right, 111 top, 113 bottom left, 120 bottom, 125 left and right, 137; City Engineers Department, Portsmouth 107; Courtauld Institute of Art, London 84 bottom; Murray-Davison, Winchester 138, 141; Mary Evans Picture Library, London 115 top; John R. Freeman & Co., London 73, 75, 114 top, 133; Hamlyn Group Picture Library 11 top and bottom, 29 top, 30, 31, 62; Hamlyn Group–Derek Balmer 37, 44, 47, 68, 80, 82, 86, 90 bottom, 91, 92 top, 94 top and bottom, 126 bottom right; Hamlyn Group–J. Butler-Kearney 17 bottom, 18 top, 19, 22, 24, 25 bottom left, 34, 35, 58, 59, 70 top, 89, 92 bottom, 93 left and right, 103 bottom left, 110 top and bottom, 113 bottom right, 115 bottom, 118, 120 top, 121, 131, 132, 139; Hamlyn Group–Sally Chappell 23, 36, 41 bottom right, 48 top left, 70 bottom, 99, 134; Hamlyn Group–John R. Freeman & Co. 13, 98, 119; Hamlyn Group–J. A. Hewes title page; Hampshire County Museum Service, Winchester 55, 66; The Mansell Collection, London 48 bottom right, 50, 65, 69, 77, 111 bottom, 127; National Film Archive, London–M.G.M. 130; National Gallery of Scotland 54; National Maritime Museum, Greenwich 114 bottom; National Monuments Record, London 87; National Portrait Gallery, London 81 bottom, 123; Philpot Museum, Lyme Regis–Gerald Silverlock 96; Radio Times Hulton Picture Library, London 10, 29 bottom, 38 top, 45, 63 top, 74, 76, 79, 81 top, 85; Royal Institute of British Architects, London 135; Sotheby Parke Bernet, London 136; Tate Gallery, London 12; Victoria and Albert Museum, London 63 bottom, 126 top left; Brian Wilks, Leeds 9, 16, 117.

The author and publishers would like to thank the following for permission to reproduce copyright material.
The Oxford University Press for R. W. Chapman's edition of *The Oxford Illustrated Jane Austen* and *Jane Austen's Letters to her sister Cassandra and Others* (2nd edition, 1952) and for *Jane Austen, Facts and Problems* (1948) and *Jane Austen, A Critical Bibliography* (2nd edition, 1953), also by R. W. Chapman; Penguin Books Ltd. for the Penguin edition of *Sanditon*; the *New Statesman* for the quotation from the article by Sir Harold Nicolson. We have also used extracts from the Steventon edition of R. A. Austen Leigh's *A Memoir of Jane Austen* published by R. Bentley, London, in 1882; from Haydn's *Third London Notebook* edited by H. C. Robbins and published by Barrie and Rockliffe; from O. E. Deutsch, *Handel: A Documentary Biography*, 1955; from Douglas Jefferson, *Jane Austen's Emma*, published by the Sussex University Press. Every reasonable effort has been made to trace all persons having any rights in the *Austen Papers* and in *Jane Austen, her Life and Letters* both by R. A. Austen Leigh, and the appropriate acknowledgment will be made in further editions upon written notification to the publishers.

Index